学前教育专业英语

（第2版）

主　编　周海茹　姜艳敏　周海昕

北京理工大学出版社
BEIJING INSTITUTE OF TECHNOLOGY PRESS

版权专有　侵权必究

图书在版编目（CIP）数据

学前教育专业英语 / 周海茹，姜艳敏，周海昕主编. —2版. -- 北京：北京理工大学出版社，2022.7
ISBN 978-7-5763-1442-7

Ⅰ.①学… Ⅱ.①周… ②姜… ③周… Ⅲ.①学前教育—英语 Ⅳ.①G613.2

中国版本图书馆CIP数据核字（2022）第114820号

出版发行 / 北京理工大学出版社有限责任公司
社　　址 / 北京市海淀区中关村南大街5号
邮　　编 / 100081
电　　话 / (010)68914775（总编室）
　　　　　(010)82562903（教材售后服务热线）
　　　　　(010)68944723（其他图书服务热线）
网　　址 / http：//www.bitpress.com.cn
经　　销 / 全国各地新华书店
印　　刷 / 北京广达印刷有限公司
开　　本 / 787毫米×1092毫米　1/16
印　　张 / 13　　　　　　　　　　　　　　　责任编辑 / 龙　微
字　　数 / 312千字　　　　　　　　　　　　　文案编辑 / 龙　微
版　　次 / 2022年7月第2版　2022年7月第1次印刷　责任校对 / 周瑞红
定　　价 / 70.00元　　　　　　　　　　　　　责任印制 / 施胜娟

图书出现印装质量问题，请拨打售后服务热线，本社负责调换

前　言

　　《学前教育专业英语》的编写旨在适应学前教育专业的发展，满足职业院校学前教育专业的课程需求。对于学前教育专业，英语课一直都是必修的公共基础课，满足学生对于英语基础知识的学习及基本技能的掌握。就职业院校而言，与职业相关的英语知识和技能也应是课程体系的组成部分，只有在公共英语课的基础上开设专业英语课，才能更好地适应职业院校的发展需要。

　　《学前教育专业英语》的设计将学前教育与英语教育的相关知识和技能有效地整合，突出"学前教育＋英语教育"的专业特色，体现职业院校英语教育的目标。本书力求所采用的素材具有专业性、实用性、真实性和实效性，贴近生活、贴近职业。同时，素材内容并不局限于英语教育，而是涵盖了学前教育的各个学科领域，具有实践上的指导性。

　　本书共 8 个单元，每个单元由 5 个功能板块组成，具体结构设计如下：

　　板块 1. Skills for Pre-school English Teaching：培养和训练学前英语教育的相关技能。其中包括英语语音的自然拼读法；幼儿教师日常教学和管理用语；经典歌曲童谣、曲谱；有趣的小故事和英语教学游戏等。幼儿教师在已有的英语知识基础上通过该板块的训练，能够掌握幼儿英语教育的教学手段和方法，提高教学能力。

　　板块 2. Pre-school Education in English：通过学习课文，掌握和积累学前教育英语词汇，了解英语句法结构，提高英语阅读理解能力；通过阅读，学习和了解世界各地学前教育行业的现状和发展，了解其他国家幼儿园各个学科领域流行的教学模式和方法，以指导今后的教学实践。

　　板块 3. English Proficiency：通过重温英语词法和句法知识，扩大英语词汇量，提高单词拼读和句法的应用能力，以在未来的学前英语词汇及句型教学中更加得心应手。

　　板块 4. Unit Practice：将本单元的重点提炼出来，做集中的练习和巩固。

　　板块 5. Extended Reading：通过拓展阅读，锻炼阅读理解能力，并了解国外幼儿园学习中心（区域或角落）设定的发展目标、操作方法和投放材料等内容，作为今后工作的参考。

　　此外，为了给教师备课提供参考，同时也为职业院校学生自学、在职幼儿教师进修学习提供方便，本书在每单元课文后配有注释（Notes）和词汇表（Useful Words and Expressions），并在最后配有课文和拓展阅读的参考译文及单元练习的参考答案。

　　本书配有二维码、课件、音频、视频等资源，多媒体视听图文并茂，形式活泼，可阅读性强。此次修订增设了"课程思政"模块，每个单元的思政点与课文内容有机融合，潜移默化进行思政教育渗透及意识形态引导。

　　本书正文全部内容及资源由周海茹、姜艳敏和周海昕共同编写和编辑。本书的编写受到营口职业技术学院及其师范教育学院领导的高度关注、大力支持与悉心指导，在此深表谢意。

　　由于作者水平和能力所限，本书的编写难免出现疏漏或不当，敬请专家、同行及读者批评指正。

编　者

目 录

UNIT 1　Child Rights ················· 1

UNIT 2　Early Years Development ·········· 21

UNIT 3　The Benefits of Playgrounds ······ 43

UNIT 4　Learning Environment I ············ 61

UNIT 5　Learning Environment II ·········· 79

UNIT 6　Pre-school Music Education ······ 97

UNIT 7　Language Development ·········· 115

UNIT 8　Teacher Handbook ················· 137

Translations and Keys ························ 157

References ················ 199

UNIT 1

Child Rights

> "There are no seven wonders of the world in the eyes of a child. There are seven million."
>
> —Walt Streightiff

Learning Objectives

Students will
★ review English phonemes
★ be familiar with school languages, chants, songs and stories
★ learn how to play a game for children
★ master new words and expressions
★ understand what an early childhood programme should look like and learn how to build up the strengths of the children
★ review conversion words and nouns

Part 1　Skills for Pre-school English Teaching

Phonemes 音素

Vowels 元音（20 个）			Consonants 辅音（28 个）		
单元音	前元音	[iː] [ɪ] [e] [æ]	爆破音	清辅音	[p] [t] [k]
				浊辅音	[b] [d] [g]
	中元音	[ɜː] [ə] [ʌ]	摩擦音	清辅音	[f] [θ] [s] [ʃ] [h]
				浊辅音	[v] [ð] [z] [ʒ] [r]
	后元音	[ɑː] [ɒ] [ɔː] [u] [uː]	鼻辅音	[m] [n] [ŋ]	
双元音	合口双元音	[eɪ] [aɪ] [ɔɪ] [au] [əu]	破擦音	清辅音	[tʃ] [tr] [ts]
				浊辅音	[dʒ] [dr] [dz]
	集中双元音	[ɪə] [eə] [uə]	舌边音	[l]	
			半元音	[w] [j]	

音素（Phoneme）是根据语音的自然属性划分出来的最小语音单位。从生理性质来看，一个发音动作形成一个音素。如 [m] 的发音动作是：上唇和下唇闭拢，声带振动，气流从鼻腔冲出发音，用语音学术语来说，就是双唇鼻音。

英语共有 48 个音素，一般分为元音（vowel）和辅音 (consonant) 两大类，其中元音 20 个，辅音 28 个。气流由肺部发出，经过口腔能自由呼出不受阻碍，而且声带颤动，这样发出的声音就是元音，如 [e]、[ə] 等；气流从肺部呼出后，经过口腔时，在一定部位受到阻碍，除浊辅音外，声带不颤动，这样发出的语音就是辅音，如 [f]、[b] 等。

元音分为单元音和双元音，按发音部位又分为前、中、后，而辅音的分类比较复杂。辅音如按发音部位分类，则有唇音、舌音等，如按发音方法分类，则有塞音、擦音、边音、鼻音等，如按发音方式分类，则有清音、浊音等。

音素不同于字母，音素依靠听觉辨别，字母依靠视觉辨认。音素是字母组合后的读音标记，它属于读音系统，字母则属于拼写系统。因此，phonetics 一词就拼写来看是由 9 个字母拼写而成的，但就读音来看只有 8 个音素。

英语辅音和元音在语言中的作用，就相当于汉语中的声母和韵母。音素一般用国际音标 International Phonetic Alphabet(IPA) 标记。国际音标是国际上通行的一种记音符号，一般用 [ ] 或 / / 标明，如 [fəˈnetɪks] 或 /fəˈnetɪks/。

School Languages

Arrivals & Dismissing 入园和离园

- Good morning. / Hello, sweetie! / Nice to meet (see) you!
  早上好！／你好，宝贝！／很高兴见到你！
- We missed you. Did you miss your friends?
  我们都想你了，你有没有想朋友们呀？
- Give me a hug / Give me five!
  抱抱我吧。／我们来击掌吧！
- How are you today? / Are you happy today?
  你今天好吗？／你今天开心吗？
- You look very / so beautiful / handsome / smart today.
  你今天看起来好漂亮／好帅／好清爽！
- I like your new dress / hairstyle.
  我喜欢你的新裙子／新发型！
- Why are you looking unhappy / sad?
  你为什么看上去不开心呢？
- Come on in! Leave your bag.
  快进来！放好书包。
- Say "good-bye" to your daddy / mummy.
  跟爸爸／妈妈说再见。
- Have fun! / Have a nice day!
  今天过得开心点儿！

- That's all for today. / So much for today. / Class dismissed.
  今天就到这里了。／下课了！
- Were you happy? / Did you have fun, today?
  你们过得开心吗？／你们今天玩得好吗？
- School is over. It's time to go home.
  放学啦！该回家了！
- Get your things done up. / Put away your things.
  把你们的事情做完。／把你们手里的东西放回去。
- Get your clothes neat. / Put on your coat.
  把衣服整理好。／穿好外衣。
- Don't forget your bag. / Take your schoolbag with you.
  别忘了拿书包。／把书包带走。
- Say "Bye-bye" to your friends.
  跟小朋友们告别吧。
- Good-bye, sweetie（honey）. / See you tomorrow（Monday）!
  再见，宝贝！／明天见！／周一见！

Chants & Songs

You Have One I Have One 拍手歌

You have one, I have one, two little children see a big bun.

You have two, I have two, four little children go to school.

You have three, I have three, six little children plant many trees.

You have four, I have four, eight little children stand at the door.

You have five, I have five, ten little children stand in a line.

YOU HAVE ONE
I HAVE ONE

TWINKLE, TWINKLE, LITTLE STAR

Words: Jane Taylor, 1806
Music: Traditional

1. Twinkle, twinkle, little star, How I wonder what you are! Up above the world so high, Like a diamond in the sky, Twinkle, twinkle, little star, How I wonder what you are.

TWINKLE, TWINKLE, LITTLE STAR

2. When the blazing sun is gone,
   When he nothing shines upon,
   Then you show your little light,
   Twinkle, twinkle, all the night,
   Twinkle, twinkle, little star,
   How I wonder what you are.

4. In the dark blue sky you keep,
   Often through my curtain peep,
   For you never shut your eye,
   Till the sun is in the sky,
   Twinkle, twinkle, little star,
   How I wonder what you are.

3. Then the traveler in the dark,
   Thanks you for your tiny spark,
   He could not see where to go,
   If you did not twinkle so,
   Twinkle, twinkle, little star,
   How I wonder what you are.

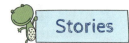

Stories

The Wind and the Sun 风和太阳

Hello, my name is Titi. When I see new friends, I want to say hello. I say, "Hello, my friend, my name is Titi." They say, "Hello Titi, nice to meet you."

One day, I saw a flower. He was alone. He had no friends. I wanted to talk to him. "Good morning. My name is Titi. What is your name?"

The flower answered, "My name is Kiki." I said, "Nice to meet you, Kiki." Kiki said, "Nice to meet you too, Titi." Kiki became my new friend.

Look for a Friend 找朋友

Sam is a fish. He lives in the sea. He is very lonely. He wants to have a friend. The friend looks like him. Sam sees an ink fish. The ink fish has eight legs. He doesn't look like Sam. So Sam goes away. Sam meets a shark. He wants to say hello to the shark. The shark opens his big mouth. Sam runs away quickly. Sam is tired and hungry. He wants to have a rest. Then he sees a round fish. She says to him. "Hello! Would you like to be my friend?" Sam answers, "Of course! But you are round. I am flat." The round fish says, "But we are both fishes." Sam thinks and says, "You are right. Let's be friends." They become good friends.

 Game

Body Alphabet 人体字母

Objective: Learn the alphabet

Teaching aids: a mat, a timer

Rules：1. The class learns how to use the limbs and trunk to act out the alphabet.

2. Divide the class into groups of three.

3. The groups take turns to come to the mat and act out the capital letters they hear as more as they can in given time.

4. The group that has done the most will be the winner.

Extension: Use the fingers to make the shapes of lowercase letters.

Language："Show me the big letter W."

"Can you guess what this letter is?"

"See which group can be the first one to make a shape of W."

"Use your finger(s) to make a small b."

"Put your small b on your head."

"Put your small b on your mouth."

"Put your b on your desk."

Part 2 Pre-school Education in English

What should an early childhood development programme look like?

Early childhood development programmes are not only about the children, they are also about influencing the contexts in which children are growing up... Programmes should build on the strengths that already exist within family, community and society. At the same time, they should work to build up the strengths of the children:

• Physical strengths: such as prenatal care and nutrition for mothers, appropriate nutrition for children; immunization; appropriate shelter; clean water; good sanitation and hygiene; opportunities and encouragement to develop gross and fine motor skills.

• Intellectual strengths: such as language acquisition and exposure to stories; activities that encourage a child to explore and be curious; understanding basic concepts such as numbers, colours, dimensions and so on; encouraging creativity and critical thinking.

• Social strengths: such as learning about one's own identity, understanding relationships in the family and neighbourhood; interacting with peers and others in accordance with accepted norms of the society; acquiring good communication skills, being able to cooperate.

• Moral and emotional strengths: such as having stable relationships, love, affection and a sense of security; understanding the belief system of family and society; learning what is wise and what is not wise; being a critical thinker; instilling and strengthening the ability to protect oneself.

The Convention presents development as a continuing process of interaction between the individual child, with his or her inherent characteristics, and the immediate and larger environment, resulting in evolving capacities and maturity... The child is an active participant, not a blank slate to be manipulated. Even the very youngest children can communicate, and it is our task, as adults, to encourage and assist them to develop their strengths and their skills...

... There are many options and many approaches. Some aspects need to be emphasized, such as the importance of programmes that support parents and families rather than replace them; such as training people from the local community to implement early childhood activities rather than insisting that all personnel be professionally qualified; such as communities, parents and children participating in decision-making about their programmes and activities...

In many countries, early childhood development programmes are initiated... or implemented by civil society organizations... It is the government's role to create an (legal, policy, social) environment that will permit and encourage the healthy development of young children and their families...

The aim is to build sustainable programmes and services that ensure that all young children have the opportunity to develop their innate potential to the greatest extent possible. That is our collective responsibility. The children cannot wait.

Notes

1. Background

The United Nations, *Convention on the Rights of the Child* is applicable with regard to all persons under the age of 18... Article 29 of *Convention on the Rights of the Child* establishes the child's right to education. However, learning and education do not begin with primary schools. They begin with responsive and stimulating adult-infant interaction... Information about early learning and development should be made widely available so that families do not miss these early opportunities. A research shows that children profit from organized early learning experiences, particularly the poorest children.

联合国的《儿童权利公约》适用于所有 18 岁以下的人。……《儿童权利公约》第 29 条确立了儿童受教育权。然而，学习和教育不是从小学开始的，是从成人与婴儿之间反应性和刺激性的互动开始的……关于早期学习和发展的信息应该被广泛应用，这样家庭就不会错过这些早期教育的机会。研究表明，儿童可从安排有序的早期学习经历中获益，尤其是最贫穷的儿童。

2. early childhood development programmes 儿童早期发展方案（计划）

3. they are also about influencing the contexts *in which* children are growing up

方案还涉及对儿童成长环境的影响

in which 引导定语从句修饰先行词 contexts

e.g. Two major areas *in which* mentally retarded children require help are memory and attention.

智障儿童主要是在记忆力和注意力这两方面需要帮助。

4. Programmes should *build on* the strengths that already exist within family, community and society.

方案应以家庭、社区和社会中已有的优势为基础来制定。

build on 以……为基础

e.g. I am determined to build on this solid foundation. 我决定在这个坚实的基础之上继续努力。

5. to develop gross and fine motor skills 发展粗大运动和精细运动技能

e.g. The study on characteristics and correlation between gross motor and fine motor skills developments in high risk infants with potential cerebral palsy of different birth weight

不同出生体重脑瘫高危儿婴儿期粗大与精细运动技能发育特征及其相关性研究

6. interacting with peers and others *in accordance with accepted* norms of the society

按照社会公认的准则与同伴及他人相处

in accordance with 与……一致，依照

e.g. We should make decisions in accordance with specific conditions.

我们应当根据具体情况做出决定。

 in accordance with its natural tendency 顺其自然

in accordance with practice [法] 按照惯例，根据实践

accepted 公认的；可以接受的（accept 的过去分词用作形容词）

7. understanding the belief system of family and society 理解家庭和社会的信仰体系

8. *The Convention* presents development as a continuing process of interaction between the individual child, with his or her inherent characteristics, and the immediate and larger environment, resulting in evolving capacities and maturity...

《公约》将发展视为一个持续的过程，即个体儿童及其固有的特性与当前以及更大的环境之间的互动过程，从而导致其能力和成熟度的不断变化。

The Convention：The United Nations' *Convention on the Rights of the Child*
联合国《儿童权利公约》

9. The child is an active participant, not a blank slate to be manipulated.
儿童是一个积极的参与者，而不是一块被操纵的空白石板。

Usefull Words and Expressions

context ['kɒntekst] n. 语境；情境；背景；环境
strength [streŋθ] n. 力量，优点，长处
prenatal [ˌpriːˈneɪtl] adj. 出生前的，胎儿期的
　　prenatal care 产前保健
nutrition [njuˈtrɪʃn] n. 营养学；营养品；营养
appropriate [əˈprəʊpriət] adj. 适当的；恰当的
immunization [ˌɪmjʊnaɪˈzeɪʃn] n. 免疫
shelter [ˈʃeltə] n. 避难所；遮蔽；居所；收容所
sanitation [ˌsænɪˈteɪʃn] n. 卫生系统或设备
hygiene [ˈhaɪdʒiːn] n. 卫生，卫生学；保健法
　　food hygiene 食品卫生
　　personal hygiene 个人卫生
acquire [əˈkwaɪə] vt. 学到；获得，取得
acquisition [ˌækwɪˈzɪʃn] n. 收购；获得
　　language acquisition 语言习得
exposure [ɪkˈspəʊʒə] n. 暴露；揭发；公开
　　exposure to stories 听故事
curious [ˈkjʊəriəs] adj. 好奇的；奇妙的；求知的
concept ['kɒnsept] n. 观念；概念；想法；总的印象
critical [ˈkrɪtɪkl] adj. 关键的，批评的，爱挑剔的
　　critical thinking 批判性思维
identity [aɪˈdentəti] n. 身份 [逻] 同一性；个性

in accordance with 与……一致；依照
norm [nɔːm] n. 规范；准则；标准；行为模式
approach [əˈprəʊtʃ] n. 方法，途径；接近
　　vt.& vi. 接近，走近，靠近
stable [ˈsteɪbl] adj. 稳定的；沉稳 [持重] 的；[物理学] 稳定平衡的；持久的
affection [əˈfekʃn] n. 喜爱，慈爱；情感或感情
wise [waɪz] adj. 聪明的，有智慧的；博学的
instill [ɪnˈstɪl] vt. <美> 逐渐使某人获得（某种可取的品质），逐步灌输
convention [kənˈvenʃn] n. 会议；全体与会者；国际公约；惯例，习俗，规矩
inherent [ɪnˈhɪərənt] adj. 天生；固有的，内在的
evolve [ɪˈvɒlv] vt. 使发展；使进化；设计，制订出
　　vi. 发展；通过进化进程发展或发生
manipulate [məˈnɪpjuleɪt] vt. 操纵；操作，处理 [医] 推拿，调整
slate [sleɪt] n. 石板；板岩，页岩；行为记录
implement [ˈɪmplɪment] vt. 实施，执行；使生效
initiate [ɪˈnɪʃieɪt] vt. 开始，创始；发起
sustainable [səˈsteɪnəbl] adj. 可持续的；可支撑的

Ideological and Political Concept

儿童教育工作者应培养和树立正确的儿童观和儿童教育观，将儿童的发展视为一个持续的过程，在这个过程中儿童是积极的参与者，而不是被操控者。因此，作为儿童的教育者，我们的任务是鼓励和帮助儿童发展自己的优势和技能，建立能够确保所有儿童都有机会最大限度发挥其先天潜能的可持续方案和服务，这是全社会的集体责任，身为儿童教育工作者更是责无旁贷。

Part 3 English Proficiency

Morphology

Word Building（Ⅰ） 构词（一）

英语构词通常分为六种方法，即转化(Conversion)、派生(Derivation)、合成(Compounding)、混合（Blending）、截短（Clipping）和首尾字母结合（Acronym）。

Conversion—转化法

Conversion is the formation of new words by converting words of one part of speech to the words of another part of speech, without changes in morphological structures. Words created are new only in a grammatical sense.

英语构词法中把一种词性用作另一种词性而词形不变的方法叫做转换法，转换的单词只是语法意义上的新词。转换法大多词义不变，但有时会有一定的转变。

Types of Conversion				
→ Nouns	Examples		→ Verbs	Examples
v. → n.	Let's go out for a *walk*. 我们到外面去散散步吧。 May I have a *look*? 我可以看一下吗？		n. → v.	Please *hand* me the book. 请把那本书递给我。 We *lunched* together. 我们在一起吃了午餐。
adj. → n.	You should be dressed in *black* at the funeral. 你在葬礼中该穿黑色衣服。		adj. → v.	We will try our best to *better* our living conditions. 我们要尽力改善我们的生活状况。
The + *adj.*= The... people	The *old* in our village are living a happy life. 我们村的老年人过着幸福的生活。		adv. → v.	Murder will *out*. （谚语）恶事终必将败露。

Noun 名词

A noun is the name of a person or a thing.
名词是用来表示人、事物、地点以及抽象事物名称的单词。

例如：人：John, sister, father
事物：water, air, sun, computer
地点：London, theater
抽象事物名称：love, happiness, imagination, hope

1. 名词的分类

	Type（类型）			Examples（示例）	
Noun 名词	Proper 专有名词			Beijing the Great Wall Smith the United Nations	
	Common 普通名词	Countable 可数	Individual 个体	man, expert, factory	
			Collective 集合	audience, class, family	
		Uncountable 不可数	Mass 物质	water, coal, rice, air, gas	
			Abstract 抽象	surprise, honour, help	

2. 名词的数

(1) 可数名词的复数构成。

词尾形式	复数变化	示例
普通名词	+s 清辅音后 [s]	lip → lips; rock → rocks; maths
	浊辅音/元音后 [z]	pen → pens; tree → trees; boy → boys;
t / d	[ts] [dz]	cat → cats; bed → beds; wood → woods
ce / se	[iz] [is]	place → places; horse → horses; face → faces; case → cases
ch /sh / s / x	+ es [iz]	watch → watches; fish → fishes（"种类"）bus → buses; box → boxes; house
辅音字母 + y	变 y 为 i + es [iz]	family → families; city → cities
f / fe	变 f / fe 为 v + es [vz]	knife → knives; leaf → leaves; life → lives
不规则变化		child → children; woman → women; mouse → mice; tooth → teeth tomato → tomatoes; potato → potatoes; hero → heroes; Negro → Negroes
单复数同形		Sheep; Chinese; Japanese; fish（"条"）; deer; means
只有复数形式		People; trousers; clothes; thanks; scissors; clothes; glasses（眼镜）

(2) 不可数名词没有复数形式。

使用规则	示例
前边不能用不定冠词	It's good **weather** for mountain climbing.
不能用数词作定语	I have two boxes of **chocolate**.
作主语时谓语动词用单数形式	Your **advice was** a great help to me.
使用量词短语表示数量	**a cup of** tea; **a piece of** news; **three bottles of** water

3. 名词所有格的表示法

使用规则		示例
有生命的人 动物；时间 货币；度量 国家，城市 机构，店铺	名词 +'s s 结尾 +'	my mother's bag; the dog's house; the worker's tool ten miles' distance; two kilos' weight; today's newspaper China's future; Shanghai's street; the hotel's entrance at the florist's; at one's wit's end（江郎才尽）； Lily and Lucy's room（共有的）； Lily's and Lucy's rooms（各自的）； Children's Day; men's room; your government's policy
无生命的事物	of + 名词	the door of our classroom; the name of the school
双重所有格	of + 名词或代词 所有格	an old friend of my father's; a picture of my sister's; a friend of her; a book of mine; a sister of her

4. 名词的用法

(1) 作主语。

The *radio* says that it may stop raining later. 广播说一会儿雨可能会停。

(2) 作表语。

My sister is a *nurse*. 我姐姐是一名护士。

(3) 作宾语。

I told him a *story*. 我给他讲了个故事。

(4) 作宾语补足语。

He named her *Jenny*. 他给她取名詹妮。

(5) 作定语。

We are discussing the *population* problem. 我们正在讨论人口问题。

名词作定语一般用单数，但也有以下例外：

　　a. 复数作定语：*sports* meeting 运动会；*students* reading-room 学生阅览室；
　　　　　　　　talks table 谈判桌；the foreign *languages* department 外语系

　　b. man, woman, gentleman 等作定语时，其单复数形式根据其所修饰的名词的单复数而定。

　　e.g. *men* workers; *women* teachers

　　c. 有些原有 s 结尾的名词，作定语时，s 保留。

　　e.g. *goods* train （货车）；*arms* produce 武器生产
　　　　customs papers 海关文件；*clothes* brush 衣刷

　　d. 数词 + 名词作定语时，这个名词一般保留单数形式。

　　e.g. *two-dozen* eggs 两打（24）个鸡蛋；a *ten-mile* walk 十里路
　　　　two hundred trees 两百棵树；a *five-year* plan 一个五年计划

(6) 作状语。

See you *Monday*. 星期一见。

(7) 与介词组成短语。

I am working hard *on my Chinese*. 我正在努力学习汉语。

(8) 作介词宾语。

Give the money to *your sister*. 把钱给你姐姐。

Article 冠词

> 冠词是虚词，本身不能单独使用，也没有词义，它用在名词的前面，帮助指明名词的含义。

1. 冠词的分类

不定冠词 The Indefinite Article	定冠词 The Definite Article	零冠词 Zero Article
a [ə] / an [ən]	the[ðə] / [ði:]	不使用冠词

2. 掌握不定冠词 a / an 的用法

（1）读音：在以辅音（音素，非字母）开头的名词前用 a，读作 [ə]：a book; a university
　　　　　在以元音（音素，非字母）开头的名词前用 an，读作 [ən]：an egg; an hour

（2）语法功能：用在可数名词的单数形式前表泛指——表明一类人或事物，区别于其他类。

I am a Chinese. 我是（一个）中国人。
A car runs faster than a bike. 汽车比自行车快。
An elephant is bigger than a horse. 大象比马大。
She wanted to rent an apartment near the campus. 她想在学校附近租一套房子。
Sally sent me a picture of herself. 萨莉送给我一张她的照片。
A grammar book is necessary to a language learner. 对语言学习者来说，语法书是很必要的。

（3）用于某些约定俗成的词组或习语中。

a little 一点儿	a great many 很多	in a word 总而言之
a few 几个	many a time 多次；常常	in a short while 不久
a lot of 许多	as a rule 一般来说	after a while 过一会儿
a type of 一种类型的	in a hurry 匆忙	keep an eye on 照看；留意
a pile of 一堆	in a minute 立刻；马上	all of a sudden 突然

3. 掌握定冠词 the 的用法

（1）读音：在以辅音（音素，非字母）开头的名词前读作 [ðə]：the book; the university
　　　　　在以元音（音素，非字母）开头的名词前读作 [ði:]：the airport; the honour

（2）语法功能：用以特指某（些）人或某（些）事物。

类型	示例
定语限定 双方明确	This is *the* house where Lu Xun once lived. 这是鲁迅曾经住过的房子。 Open *the* door, please. 请把门打开。
上文提过 再次提到	Once there lived a lion in the forest. Every day *the* lion asked small animals to look for food for him. 从前森林里住着一只狮子。每天这只狮子要小动物们为他寻找食物。 （第一次提到用不定冠词 a / an；再次提到用定冠词 the。）

其他用法	示例
序数词 形容词最高级	January is **the first** month of the year. 一月份是一年当中的第一个月。 The Potala Palace is **the highest** palace in the world. 布达拉宫是世界上海拔最高的宫殿。
宇宙中独一无二	**the** sun 太阳；**the** earth 地球；**the** sky 天空；**the** world 世界
方向、方位	in **the** east 在东方，in **the** front 在前面，on **the** right 在右边
专有名词	**The** United Nations 联合国；**The** Communist Party 共产党 **The** Pacific Ocean 太平洋；**The** Spring Festival 春节
姓氏复数指一家人	**The Bakers** came to see me yesterday. 贝克一家人昨天来看我。
在某些形容词前，使其名词化，指一类人或物	**the** poor 穷人；**the** rich 富人；**the** sick 病人；**the** wounded 伤员 **the** good 好人；**the** beautiful 美丽的事物
强调语气 固定结构	This is **the** very book I want. 这就是我想要的那本书。 **The** more we get together, **the** happier we'll be. 我们相聚越多越快乐。
演奏西洋乐器	play **the** piano 弹钢琴；play **the** violin 拉小提琴
身体某一部位	take sb. by **the** arm 抓住某人的手臂；hit sb. in **the** face 打某人的脸 be red in **the** face 脸红；be lame in **the** right leg 右腿瘸
某些固定的表达法	in **the** morning 在早上；go to **the** cinema 去看电影 go to **the** theatre 去看戏；on **the** way to 前往……的路上

4. 掌握零冠词的用法

零冠词是指名词前面没有不定冠词、定冠词，也没有其他限定词的现象。

泛指的不可数／复数名词	**Books** are my best friends. 书是我最好的朋友。 **Water** boils at 100℃. 水在 100℃沸腾。	
人名；地名；国名	**Lu Xun** is a great Chinese writer. 鲁迅是一位伟大的中国作家。 **London** is the capital of England. 伦敦是英国的首都。 **China** is a developing country. 中国是一个发展中国家。	
季节；月份；星期；节假日	**Summer** begins in June here. 这儿的夏天从六月份开始。 There are a lot of people shopping at **Christmas**. 在圣诞节有很多人购买东西。 We have no classes on **Sunday**. 星期日我们不上课。	
三餐饭菜／语言／游戏／运动／项目	have **supper** 吃晚饭 She speaks **Chinese**. 她说汉语。 He plays **football**. 他踢足球。 Let's have a game of **chess**. 咱俩下盘棋吧。	
固定结构 改变原意	go to school（to study）去上学 in church（to worship）做礼拜 in hospital 住院（治疗） in prison 服刑	go to the school（spot）去学校（地点） in the church（spot）在教堂（地点） in the hospital 在医院 in the prison 在监狱
职位／头衔／身份	Professor Wang 王教授；Doctor Tompson 汤普生医生 President Lincoln 林肯总统；Dean of the English Department 英语系主任	

Part 4 Unit Practice

1. Read aloud the phonemes and fill out the form.

[i:] [e] [æ] [ɑ:] [ɜ:] [ɪ] [u:] [ə] [ʌ] [ɒ] [ɔ:] [u] [eɪ] [aɪ] [eə] [əu] [uə] [ɔɪ] [ɪə] [au]

[p] [tʃ] [w] [k] [b] [v] [ŋ] [d] [g] [f] [dʒ] [θ] [t] [j] [s] [ts] [ʃ] [h] [ð] [z] [ʒ] [r] [m] [n] [dr] [tr] [dz] [l]

Vowels 元音（20个）		Consonants 辅音（28个）	
单元音	前元音	爆破音	清辅音
			浊辅音
	中元音	摩擦音	清辅音
			浊辅音
	后元音	鼻辅音	
双元音	合口双元音	破擦音	清辅音
			浊辅音
		舌边音	
	集中双元音	半元音	

2. Put the school languages into English.

早上好，宝贝！   你有没有想我们？   把你们的事情做完。

你今天看起来很棒！   今天就到这里了。下课！   请把书包带走。

快进来！把书包放下。   你们今天过得开心吗？   周一见！明天见！

3. Put the following phrases and sentences into Chinese.

(1) language acquisition

(2) exposure to stories

(3) interacting with peers and others in accordance with accepted norms of the society

(4) Even the very youngest children can communicate.

(5) It is our task, as adults, to encourage and assist them to develop their strengths and their skills.

(6) Communities, parents and children participate in decision-making about their programmes and activities.

4. Match the sentences with conversion words and the type of conversion.

v. → n.　　　　We will try our best to **better** our living.

adj. → n.　　　Murder will **out**.

n. → v.　　　　I think we'd better finish the **talk** now.

adj. → v.　　　We don't belong to the **rich**, but we don't belong to the **poor** either.

adv. → v.　　　The girl in **black** appears very beautiful.

The + adj.　　 **Hand** in your papers, please.

5. Chose the best answer to complete the sentences.

(1) As he reached _____ front door, Jack saw _____ strange sight.

　　A. the; /　　　B. a; the　　　C. /; a　　　D. the; a

(2) In communication, a smile is usually _____ strong sign of a friendly and _____ open attitude.
   A. the; /   B. a; an   C. a; /   D. the; an

(3) —It's said John will be in a job paying over $60,000 _____ year.
   —Right, he will also get paid by _____ week.
   A. the; the   B. a; the   C. the; a   D. a; a

(4) Anyway, I can't cheat him—it's against all my _____.
   A. emotions   B. principles   C. regulations D. opinions

(5) The lack of ecofriendly habits among the public is thought to be a major _____ of global climate change.
   A. result   B. cause   C. warning   D. reflection

(6) What's the _____, in your opinion, of helping him if he doesn't make an effort to help himself?
   A. sympathy   B. theme   C. object   D. point

(7) Always remember to put such dangerous things as knives out of children's _____.
   A. touch   B. sight   C. reach   D. distance

(8) "Tommy, run! Be quick! The house is on fire!" the mother shouted, with _____ clearly in her voice.
   A. anger   B. rudeness   C. regret   D. panic

Part 5 Extended Reading

About UNICEF

UNICEF is the United Nations International Children's Fund. Our mandate from the United Nations General Assembly is to help children around the world realize their rights to survival, development, protection and participation. UNICEF works in 190 countries and territories to protect the rights of every child. UNICEF has spent 70 years working to improve the lives of children and their families. Defending children's rights throughout their lives requires a global presence, aiming to produce results and understand their effects. UNICEF promotes the rights and wellbeing of every child, in everything we do. Together with our partners, we work in 190 countries and territories to translate that commitment into practical action, focusing special effort on reaching the most vulnerable and excluded children, to the benefit of all children, everywhere.

The State of the World's Children 2016: A fair chance for every child

   Every child has the right to health, education and protection, and every society has a stake in expanding children's opportunities in life. Yet, around the world, millions of children are denied a fair chance for no reason other than the country, gender or circumstances into which they are born. *The State of the World's Children* 2016 argues that progress for the most disadvantaged children is not only a moral, but also a strategic imperative. Stakeholders have a clear choice to make: invest in accelerated progress for the children being left behind, or face the consequences of a far more divided world by 2030. At the start of a new development agenda, the report concludes with a set of recommendations to help chart the course towards a more equitable world.

> **Education Is the Key to Opportunities**
> UNICEF believes that quality education is a right for all children, whether in the developing world or amidst conflict and crisis.

Life's early years have a profound impact on a child's future. When loved, nourished and cared for in safe and stimulating environments, children develop the skills they need to embrace opportunity and bounce back from adversity. But nearly 43% of children under 5 in low- and middle-income countries are not getting the nutrition, protection and stimulation they need. This diminishes both the child's potential and sustainable growth for society at large.

The good news is that early childhood presents an incomparable window of opportunity to make a difference in a child's life. The right interventions at the right time can counter disadvantage and boost a child's development.

Across the world, UNICEF's early childhood development programmes offer interventions that combine nutrition, protection and stimulation and support parents, caregivers and communities – to help vulnerable children get a fair start in life.

Wang Yuan, appointed UNICEF Special Advocate for Education, will support the promotion of high quality education for every child

BEIJING, 28 June 2017—Well-known Chinese singer and actor, a member of the pop band TFBOYS, Wang Yuan was today appointed by United Nations International Children's Fund (UNICEF) as Special Advocate for Education.

UNICEF China Acting Representative Dr. Douglas Noble and the well-known Chinese singer and actor, a member of the pop band TFBOYS, Wang Yuan, showcase a UNICEF Special Advocate for Education appointment letter at an event at UNICEF's Beijing Office on 28 June, 2017.

"I am very proud to join UNICEF China as Special Advocate for Education. It's not only an honour but also a responsibility. From this day on, I will be more active in promoting education and development for China's children, and do as much practical work as I can... Education is a right; we should never allow it to be a privilege. Let's work hard to make education even better in the future." Wang Yuan remarked at the announcement event at UNICEF's Beijing Office.

UNICEF works with the Government of China to promote and support high quality education for all of China's children. It works with partners to implement Child Friendly School model in remote and disadvantaged areas of China. A child friendly school is one that is designed for the best interests of the child. UNICEF believes that children come first and every child, no matter who they are, no matter what part of China they come from, has a right to receive high quality education.

"It is my great pleasure to welcome Wang Yuan as a Special Advocate for Education for UNICEF China," said Dr. Douglas Noble, UNICEF China Acting Representative. "We are thankful to Wang Yuan for joining us in this important endeavor to promote high quality education for every child. We look forward to continued collaboration– with our partners, with all the hard-working teachers and students, in promoting, protecting and fulfilling the rights of all children in China."

Wang Yuan will visit the UNICEF-supported Child Friendly School project in the remote rural communities in China, support awareness raising programmes and appear at key public events.

Chinese singer and actor, a member of the pop band TFBOYS, Wang Yuan shares his thoughts on quality education with 10 students from a primary school in suburban Beijing following an event in UNICEF China's Beijing Office, where he was appointed as UNICEF Special Advocate for Education, on 28 June, 2017.

For more information about UNICEF and its work：
Visit: http://www.unicef.org
Visit UNICEF China website: http://www.unicef.cn
Follow us on Sina Weibo: http://weibo.com/unicefchina
Wechat: unicefchina

Early Years Development

> It is the supreme art of the teacher to awaken joy in creative expression and knowledge.
>
> —Albert Einstein

Learning Objectives

Students will
- ★ review alphabet sounds
- ★ be familiar with school languages, chants, songs and stories
- ★ learn how to play a game for children
- ★ master new words and expressions
- ★ understand the influence play has over the development of children and learn how to create opportunities for children's play
- ★ review derivation words and pronouns

Part 1 Skills for Pre-school English Teaching

English Phonics（Ⅰ） 自然拼读法（一）

Alphabet Sounds 字母的自然读音

字母 Alphabet	名称音 Name	自然读音及单词示例 Sounds & Examples	字母 Alphabet	名称音 Name	自然读音及单词示例 Sounds & Examples
Aa	[eɪ]	[æ] apple bag rat	Nn	[en]	[n] nine nose now
Bb	[biː]	[b] ball big book	Oo	[əu]	[ɒ] box clock ox
Cc	[siː]	[k] cat class cut	Pp	[piː]	[p] map pig put
Dd	[diː]	[d] doctor good	Qq	[kjuː]	[kw] queen quick
Ee	[iː]	[e] elephant get	Rr	[ɑː]	[r] rat red rose
Ff	[ef]	[f] five food fun	Ss	[es]	[s] snake sister
Gg	[dʒiː]	[g] gate big girl	Tt	[tiː]	[t] tiger rabbit
Hh	[eɪtʃ]	[h] have horse	Uu	[juː]	[ʌ] umbrella but
Ii	[aɪ]	[ɪ] insect it sit	Vv	[viː]	[v] very five give
Jj	[dʒeɪ]	[dʒ] jump jacket	Ww	[ˈdʌblju:]	[w] water we wait
Kk	[keɪ]	[k] kitchen snake	Xx	[eks]	[ks] box exercise
Ll	[el]	[l] blue bottle	Yy	[waɪ]	[j][ɪ] yellow happy
Mm	[em]	[m] monkey come	Zz	[ziː][zed]	[z] zebra zip zoo

  英语是拼音文字，所有的词汇都是由字母表中不同的字母组成的，而在成千上万的不同拼写组合中，基本发音音素却只有48个，这说明26个字母与基本音素间是有着一定关联的。但是必须指出，26个字母与基本音素之间并不是简单的一一对应关系，这说明准确掌握英语词汇的拼读并不容易。尽管如此，人们还是总结出了很多字母及字母组合的发音规律，这些规律对于绝大多数英文词汇都是适用的，这就是自然拼读法 Phonics，即看词读音，听音拼词。

  在美国及很多以英语为第一语言的国家，自然拼读法也是儿童语言启蒙所采用的教学方法。从幼儿园开始就开始按照"六阶成功法"的自然过程逐步学习：

  第一阶：建立字母与字母自然发音之间的直接联系。

第二阶：能够成功拼读元音＋辅音（辅音＋元音），如：a-t → at。
第三阶：能够成功拼读辅音＋元音＋辅音，如：d-o-g → dog。
第四阶：能够成功拼读双音节或多音节单词，如：sw-ea-t-er → sweater。
第五阶：能够听音辨词，即听到单词读音就能拼出该单词。
第六阶：大量扩充单词量，能够阅读英语文章。

School Languages

Morning Roll Call 早点名

- Let's call the roll./Let's have a roll call.
  我们来点名。
- Answer when your name is called.
  点到名字的请回答。
- Please stand up and say "here / I'm here."
  请站起来说"到"。
- Is everyone here? / Are we all here?
  人都到齐了吗?
- Who is not here? / Who is absent?
  谁缺席了?
- What day is today? / Who is on duty today?
  今天星期几? / 今天谁值日?
- What's the weather like today?
  今天天气怎么样?
- It's fine / sunny/cloudy/windy/cold/hot.
  今天天气好（晴天；阴天；风大；冷；热）。
- What's happening?/What's the matter?
  发生了什么事? / 怎么了?
- Does anyone know?
  有人知道吗?
- I'm very glad to hear that!
  听到这个消息我很高兴！

Rhyme Time 律动

- Let's do the rhyme.
  我们来做律动吧。
- Let's share a nice chant.
  我们一起唱一首优美的歌谣。
- First say the words with me.
  先跟我一起说歌词。
- Beat time to the music with your hands.
  用手随着乐曲打拍子。
- Follow me and act with the music.
  跟我一起随着音乐做动作。

Chants & Songs

ABC Phonics Chant 字母读音歌

Ready? Let's Go!

Aa, /æ/, /æ/, apple;

Cc, /k/, /k/, cat;

Ee, /e/, /e/, elephant;

Gg, /g/, /g/, gorilla;

Ii, /ɪ/, /ɪ/, igloo;

Kk, /k/, /k/, key;

Mm, /m/, /m/, mouse;

Oo, /ɒ/, /ɒ/, octopus;

Qq, /kw/, /kw/, queen;

Ss, /s/, /s/, sock;

Uu, /ʌ/, /ʌ/, umbrella;

Ww, /w/, /w/, watch;

Yy, /j/, /j/, yacht;

Bb, /b/, /b/, book;

Dd, /d/, /d/, dog;

Ff, /f/, /f/, fish;

Hh, /h/, /h/, hat;

Jj, /dʒ/, /dʒ/, jacket;

Ll, /l/, /l/, lion;

Nn, /n/, /n/, nut;

Pp, /p/, /p/, panda;

Rr, /r/, /r/, ring;

Tt, /t/, /t/, tiger;

Vv, /v/, /v/, violin;

Xx, /ks/, /ks/, box;

Zz, /z/, /z/, zebra

All right!

Good job!

You did it!

The more we get together
我们常相聚

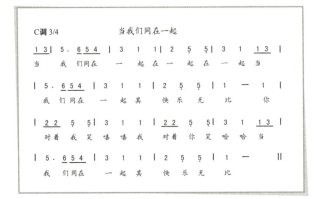

Stories

We Are the Best 我们都是最棒的

One day, the eyes, the nose, and the ears were fighting.
The eyes said, "I am the best. I can see everything!"
The nose said, "I am the best. I can smell everything!"
The ears said, "I am the best. I can hear everything!"
Then the face said, "I am the best." "Without me, you can't see anything." "You can't smell anything. You can't hear anything."
"We are the best."

We Will Do Everything Together 我们什么都一起做

I have a little brother. We will do everything together. We will do everything together. We will wake up early. We will eat breakfast together. I will share my scramble eggs with him. We will do everything together. We will get dressed together. I will dress him in my favorite shirt. We will do everything together. We will go to school together. I will let him sit behind me on my bicycle. We will do everything together. We will have bath together. I will scrub his back. We will do everything together. We will go to bed together. We will have a pillow fight. There are so many things we can do together, but first he has to learn how to walk.

Game

Numbers Huddle 数字抱团

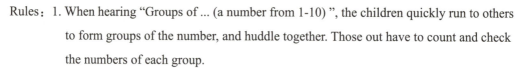

Objective: Learn the numbers

Teaching aid: flash cards

Rules：1. When hearing "Groups of ... (a number from 1-10)", the children quickly run to others to form groups of the number, and huddle together. Those out have to count and check the numbers of each group.

2. The class sit in a big circle, with flash cards of numbers (1-10) in hands. When hearing "a group of number ... (1-10)", children with the right number cards quickly get up and huddle together in the middle of the circle. Those get up with the wrong number or those never get up with the right number are out.

Extension: As to Step 2, the flash cards can be any picture cards of English words.

Part 2 Pre-school Education in English

Early Years Development Frame

Play as Learning

Children grow and develop through play. Young children, especially infants and toddlers explore the world with their five senses. They use their sight, smell, touch, hearing and taste to make sense of their physical environment, objects and the people around them. Different types of play foster different types of development in young children—physical, linguistic, cognitive, social and emotional.

Play time is more than toy time. Playing involves people, objects, or movement. Everything, from shaking rattles, pushing a cart to blowing bubbles, singing songs, splashing in the tub, chasing each other around the room, and pretending to be different characters, qualifies as play. Through play, young children learn to make friends, cooperate, communicate, solve problems and demonstrate a host of other intellectual, emotional and social behaviours. They become avid explorers, discoverers and meaning-makers.

The influence play has over the development of children is holistic and all-encompassing. Types of play include object play, sensory motor play, social play and dramatic play. Young children need the freedom and space to play, move and practise their emerging skills through various activities. They could be engaged in different types of activities, which call for varying movements—walking, tumbling, bouncing, crawling, climbing, jumping, balancing and even maneuvering bends. These movement activities could also include toys, materials and equipment. Large light weight blocks allow toddlers to practise gross motor skills as they carry them around and build structures, while balls are versatile for kicking, throwing, catching and rolling.

Social and Dramatic Play

Dramatic play helps children to understand themselves in relation to the world around them. When children engage in dramatic or imaginative play, they learn to negotiate different situations and roles, express their feelings and ideas, develop friendships, think creatively, solve problems, develop gross and fine motor skills and practise oral communication.

In early dramatic play, toddlers typically focus their play on experiences that are familiar and meaningful to them. They frequently imitate adult behaviours and may use real or realistic objects as props for dressing up, cooking and rocking the baby. However, as children develop and begin to acquire the capacity to think

symbolically, they become more adept at substituting real objects with words and actions. Older children may take on different social roles as Mummy, Daddy, baby, doctor, teacher and so on.

Educarers can create opportunities for dramatic play that are child-initiated and spontaneous by equipping play areas with a variety of props. Some of these are stuffed toys, dolls, vehicles, telephones, dress-up clothes, mirror, stoves, pots and pans, and furniture. Rotate props periodically to maintain and stimulate children's interest.

Notes

1. Background

In 2002, the Ministry of Education (MOE) Singapore launched Nurturing Early Learners (NEL): A Framework for a Kindergarten Curriculum. The Kindergarten Framework provides a broad set of principles and practices to guide early childhood educarers to plan and implement developmental appropriate activities for children aged 4 to 6 years old in kindergartens and child care centres. In 2010, The Ministry of Community Development, Youth and Sports (MCYS) initiated the Early Years Development Framework (EYDF) to provide a strong and holistic foundation for children aged 3 years and below. Together with the NEL, the two frameworks provide educarers with continuity for the care and development of children from infancy through the kindergarten years until they enter primary school.

2002 年，新加坡教育部启动了对早期学习者的培养 (NEL)：幼儿园课程框架。该幼儿园框架提供了一套广泛的原则和做法，指导幼儿保育人员为在幼儿园和幼儿保育中心的 4~6 岁的幼儿制定和实施适合幼儿发展的活动。2010 年，社区发展、青年和体育部发起了"早期发展框架"(EYDF)，为 3 岁及以下的幼儿提供一个强大而全面的基础。连同幼儿园课程框架一起，这两个框架一起为教育保育人员提供了对幼儿护理及幼儿从婴儿期、经过幼儿园期直至进入小学的发展连续性。

2. Early Years Development Frame 早期发展框架

The Early Years Development Frame is targeted at young children 3 years and below. In child care centres they would come under the following age groups: Infants: 2 to 17 months; Toddlers: 13 to 30 months; Nursery: 31 to 36 months.

早期发展框架是针对 3 岁及以下低龄儿童的。在幼儿保育中心，他们将归入下列年龄组：

婴儿（宝宝班）：2~17 个月；

幼儿（豆豆班）：13~30 个月；

托儿（苗苗班）：31~36 个月。

3. They use their sight, smell, touch, hearing and taste to make sense of their *physical environment*, objects and the people around them.

他们利用他们的视觉、嗅觉、触觉、听觉和味觉来了解周围的环境、物体和人。

physical environment 物理环境，物质环境，自然环境

e.g. Dining surrounding is equal to the physical environment and the cultural atmosphere it conveys.

饮食环境包括物质环境和人文环境两部分。

4. Different types of play foster different types of development in young children—physical, linguistic, cognitive, social and emotional.

不同类型的游戏可以在不同的方面，如生理上、语言上、认知上、社交上和情感上促进儿童的发展。

5. Play time is *more than* toy time. 玩耍时间不只是玩玩具的时间。

more than 超过；不只是；很；在……次以上

e.g. Now, if it was me, I'd want to do more than just change the locks.

不过，如果是我，我要做的就不仅仅是换锁了。

6. Everything, from shaking rattles, pushing a cart to blowing bubbles, singing songs, splashing in the tub, chasing each other around the room, and pretending to be different characters, *qualifies as* play.

一切的一切，从摇摇铃、推车，到吹泡泡、唱歌、在浴缸里玩水、在房间里互相追逐、假扮不同的人物，都可算作玩耍。

Syntactical analysis：Everything, from ... to ..., qualifies as play.（主语 + 插入语 + 谓语）

qualify as ... 通过考试等取得当……的资格；把……描述为……

e.g. An expenditure for clothing will qualify as a trade or business expense.

服装费将可算作贸易或商务开支。

7. They become avid explorers, discoverers and *meaning-makers*.

他们成为狂热的探险家、发现者和意义建构者。

meaning-makers 意义建构者

e.g. Constructivism emphasizes the importance of what the learner brings to any learning situation as an active meaning-maker and problem-solver.

建构主义强调学习者将自身经验带进学习过程、强调学习者作为积极的意义建构者和问题的解决者。

8. The *influence* play has *over* the development of children is holistic and all-encompassing.

玩耍对儿童发展的影响是整体性和全方位的。

Syntactical analysis：play has 是省略了关系代词 which/that 的定语从句，修饰先行词 influence。

influence over 对……有影响

e.g. A teacher's behavior has influence over the students. 一个老师的行为举止对学生会构成影响。

9. Educarers can create opportunities for dramatic play that are child-initiated and spontaneous by equipping play areas with a variety of props.

保教人员可以通过在表演区配备多种多样道具的方式来创造幼儿主导的、自发的戏剧表演机会。

Educare referred to as educational care, has become a new and comprehensive service that should provide pre-school children with integrated education and care...

被称为教育保健的 Educare，已成为一项为学前儿童提供综合教育和护理的新的全面服务……

Usefull Words and Expressions

frame [freɪm] *n.* 框架；构架
infant [ˈɪnfənt] *n.* 婴儿，幼儿，初学者，生手
toddler [ˈtɒdlə] *n.* 蹒跚行走的人；学步的幼儿
nursery [ˈnɜːsəri] *n.* 苗圃；婴儿室，幼儿园
foster [ˈfɒstə] *v.* 培养；促进；抚育；代养
linguistic [lɪŋˈgwɪstɪk] *adj.* 语言的；语言学的
cognitive [ˈkɒgnətɪv] *adj.* 认知的；认识的
emotional [ɪˈməʊʃənl] *adj.* 情绪的；易激动的
involve [ɪnˈvɒlv] *vt.* 包含，使参与，牵涉
rattle [ˈrætl] *n.* 嘎嘎声，嘎嘎响的儿童玩具
 shake rattles 摇摇铃
splash [splæʃ] *vt.& vi.* 溅，泼，用……使液体飞溅
tub [tʌb] *n.* 桶；澡盆；矿车
character [ˈkærəktə] *n.* 性格；角色；特点
qualify [ˈkwɒlɪfaɪ] *v.* 使具有资格；取得资格
demonstrate [ˈdemənstreɪt] *vt.* 证明；展示
a host of 许多，一大群
avid [ˈævɪd] *adj.* 热心的；贪婪的；渴望的
holistic [həʊˈlɪstɪk] *adj.* 全盘的，整体的
all-encompassing [ˈɔːlenˈkʌmpəsɪŋ] *adj.* 包罗万象的
sensory [ˈsensəri] *adj.* 感觉的，感官的
 sensory motor play 感觉运动游戏
dramatic [drəˈmætɪk] *adj.* 戏剧的，戏剧性的
 dramatic play （戏剧）表演游戏
emerge [ɪˈmɜːdʒ] *vi.* 浮现；摆脱；暴露
 emerging skills 新技能
engage in 参加，从事，忙于
call for 要求；需要；呼吁；邀请；为……叫喊
tumble [ˈtʌmbl] *vi.* 摔倒；倒塌；滚动；打滚

bounce [baʊns] *vi.* 跳，反弹；急促地动
maneuver [məˈnuːvə] *v.& n.* 机动；操纵；移动
blocks [ˈblɒks] *n.* （block 的复数）街区；积木
structure [ˈstrʌktʃə] *n.* 结构；构造；建筑物
versatile [ˈvɜːsətaɪl] *adj.* 多功能的
imaginative [ɪˈmædʒɪnətɪv] *adj.* 富于想象的；有创造力的
negotiate [nɪˈgəʊʃieɪt] *vi.* 谈判，协商，交涉
 vt. 谈判达成；成功越过
oral [ˈɔːrəl] *adj.* 口服的；口头的；口述的
typically [ˈtɪpɪkəli] *adv.* 通常；典型地；代表性地
meaningful [ˈmiːnɪŋfl] *adj.* 有意义的
imitate [ˈɪmɪteɪt] *vt.* 模仿，效仿；仿造，伪造
realistic [ˌriːəˈlɪstɪk] *adj.* 现实的；逼真的
prop [prɒp] *n.* 道具；支柱，支撑物；支持者
 vt. 支撑，支持，维持
capacity [kəˈpæsəti] *n.* 能力；容量；地位
substitute [ˈsʌbstɪtjuːt] *vt.& vi.* 代替，替换
 n. 替代物；代替者；替补
spontaneous [spɒnˈteɪniəs] *adj.* 自发的；自然的
initiate [ɪˈnɪʃieɪt] *vt.* 开始，创始；发起
 child-initiated 儿童自发的，儿童发起的
stuffed [stʌft] *adj.* 塞满了的；已经喂饱了的
pots and pans 锅碗瓢盆，坛坛罐罐，炊事用具
rotate [rəʊˈteɪt] *vi.* 旋转；循环
 vt. 使轮流轮换；交替
periodically [ˌpɪəriˈɒdɪkli] *adv.* 周期性地
stimulate [ˈstɪmjuleɪt] *vt.* 刺激，激励，鼓舞
take on ... role 承担……角色

Ideological and Political Concept

  儿童的成长和发展离不开游戏和玩耍。低龄儿童，尤其婴儿和幼儿是用他们的五感去探索世界的。保教和幼教工作者要认真执行《幼儿园教育指导纲要》和《3-6岁儿童学习与发展指南》，本着以幼儿为中心的原则，通过设计符合教育目标的游戏活动，创造幼儿主导的、自发性的游戏机会，从而专业且富有爱心和耐心地引导幼儿去探索世界。

Part 3 English Proficiency

Word Building (II) 构词（二）

Derivation I—派生法（一）

Derivation is the process of forming words by adding derivational affixes to stems. It is also called affixation. Words formed in this way are derivatives.

英语构词法中通过在词根前面加前缀或在词根后面加后缀，从而构成一个新词的方法叫做派生法。

Prefix—前缀

除少数前缀外，一般来说，英语单词的前缀只改变词的意义，不改变其词类。

	Meaning	Type	Examples
否定	不，无非，少	in-, im-, il-, ir-; un-; non-（in-; un-; 不表示否定）	**in**efficient 无效率的；**im**possible 不可能的；**il**literate 无文化的；**ir**regular 不规则的；**un**pleasant 不愉快的；**un**do 复原；**non**sense 废话；**non**stop 直达的
			同义或近义：coming / **in**coming 来到；habit / **in**habit 居住于；loose / **un**loose 解开，释放；rip / **un**rip 撕开……
	分，无	de-; dis-	**de**frost 除霜，**de**-escalate 降低，**dis**appear 消失，**dis**count 折价，**dis**order 杂乱
轻蔑	坏，错伪，假	mal-; mis-; pseudo-	**mal**function 故障，**mis**lead 误导，**pseudo**graph 伪造文件 **mis**behavior 品行不端；**mal**treat 虐待；**pseudo**nym 假名
程度尺度	大，小过低超，合	magni-; micro-; mini-; over-; sub-; under-; super-; extra-; co-;	**magni**fy 夸大，**magni**tude 重大；**micro**scope 显微镜，**micro**wave 微波；**mini**bus 小型巴士；**mini**-bar 迷你酒吧，**over**anxious 过度焦虑的；**over**work 操劳过度；**sub**conscious 潜意识；**sub**standard 不够标准；**super**natural 超自然的，**super**market 超市，**extra**ordinary 非凡的；**co**-education 男女合校制；**co**operate 合作
立场	反，对	anti-; contra-; counter-	**anti**-war 反战的；**anti**-music 非正统音乐；**contra**diction 矛盾；**counter**act 抵消；**counter**attack 反击
时间顺序	前后再	ex-; fore-; post-; pre-; re-	**ex**-president 前总统，**ex**-husband 前夫；**fore**father 祖先；**fore**cast 预测，**post**-election 竞选后；**post**-war 战后；**pre**-school 学前；**pre**-war 战前；**re**call 回忆；**re**arrangement 再安排
数字数量	单，一双，两三，五十，多千，半	mono-; bi-; tri-; pent(a)-; dec(a)-; poly-; multi-; kilo-; semi-	**mon**oxide 一氧化物，**mono**lingual 单语的，**bi**monthly 每两月一次的，**bi**lingual 双语的，**tri**cycle 三轮车，**tri**angle 三角形，**penta**gon 五角形，**penta**thlon 五项全能，**deca**thlon 十项全能，**deca**de 十年，**poly**glot 通晓多国语言的人，**poly**gon 多边形，**multi**-lateral 多边的，**multi**-purpose 多目标的，**kilo**meter 千米，**kilo**gram 千克，**semi**circle 半圆，**semi**skilled 半熟练的

33

Pronoun 代词

代词是代替名词或一句话的一种词类。大多数代词具有名词和形容词的功能。英语中的代词，按其意义、特征及在句中的作用分为：人称代词、物主代词、指示代词、反身代词、相互代词、疑问代词、关系代词、连接代词和不定代词 9 种。以下主要介绍其中 4 种。

1. 人称代词的主格和宾格

人称代词可用作主语、表语、宾语以及介词宾语。

人称 \ 数格		单数		复数	
		主格	宾格	主格	宾格
第一人称		I	me	we	us
第二人称		you			
第三人称	他	he	him	they	them
	她	she	her		
	它	it			
	不定	one		ones	

作主语（主格）：
- *I* often go shopping on Sundays. 星期日我常去购物。
- *You* are a good teacher. 你是一位优秀教师。
- *She* is a little girl. 她是一个小女孩。
- *It*'s a heavy box, *I* can't carry it. 这是一个重盒子，我搬不动。
- Shall *we* start now? 我们现在开始吗？
- Where have *they* gone? 他们去哪儿了？
- That's *it*. 就那么回事。
- It's *he*! 是他！

作宾语（宾格）作表语：
- Who teaches *you* English this year? 今年谁教你们英语？（动宾）
- Don't tell *him* about it. 不要告诉他这件事情。（动宾；介宾）
- I'm always ready to help *them*. 我随时都在准备帮助他们。（动宾）
- Our teacher is very strict with *us*. 我们的老师对我们很严格。（介宾）
- We often write letters to *her*. 我们常给她写信。（介宾）
- I saw *her* with *them*. 我看到她和他们在一起。（动宾；介宾）
- Help *me*! 救救我！（动宾）
- —Who is *it*? 谁？（表）
- —It's *me*. 是我！（表）

不同含义：
- *We* shall do our best to help the poor. 我们将尽全力帮助贫困者。
  （we 指 you and me, 表示拉近关系）
- I live in China. *She* is a great country. 我住在中国。她是一个伟大的国家。
  （she 指 beloved 心爱的，用以表达情感）
- *They* say you are good at computers. 他们说你精通计算机。
  （they 指 people，表示公认的）

2. 形容词性物主代词和名词性物主代词

表示所有关系的代词叫做物主代词。物主代词可分为形容词性物主代词和名词性物主代词两种。

名称＼形式	我的	你的	他的	她的	它的	我们的	你们的	他们的
形容词性物主代词	my	your	his	her	its	our	your	their
名词性物主代词	mine	yours	his	hers	its	ours	yours	theirs

（1）形容词性物主代词可用作定语，后边必须跟着它所修饰的名词。名词性物主代可用作主语、宾语、表语。

类别		用法示例
形容词性物主代词	定语	I love **my** country. 我热爱我的国家。Is this **your** car? 这是你的汽车吗？ Is that **her** umbrella? 那是她的伞吗？ They are **their** books. 那些是他们的书。
名词性物主代词	主语	Your classroom is very big, but **ours** is rather small. 你们的教室很大，但我们的相当小。
	宾语	**She** likes my house. I don't like **hers**. 她喜欢我的房子，我不喜欢她的。 You have your own pencil, don't take **mine**. 你有自己的铅笔，不要拿我的。
	表语	These books are **ours**. 这些书是我们的。 Whose bag is it? It's **hers**. 这是谁的书包？是她的。
双重所有格		Yesterday I met *a friend of mine* in the street. 昨天我在街上碰见了我的一位朋友。

（2）反身代词的构成和用法：反身代词在句中主要起强调作用，可用作宾语，表语，主语的同位语和宾语的同位语。用作宾语时表示强调或主语动作反射回主语；用作同位语时表示强调"本人，自己"。

分类	第一人称	第二人称	第三人称		
单数	myself	yourself	himself	herself	itself
复数	ourselves	yourselves	themselves		

e.g. Don't play with the knife, you might hurt **yourself**. 不要玩刀子，那会割伤你的。（反射）

The story *itself* is good. Only he didn't tell it well. 故事本身是好的，只是他没有讲好。（强调）

You should ask the children **themselves**. 你应该问一问孩子们自己。（强调）

3. 不定代词的基本用法

没有明确指定代替任何特定名词或形容词的词叫做不定代词，不定代词代替名词或形容词，在句中可用作主语、宾语、表语和定语。

常用不定代词如下：some, any, no, every, all, each, both, much, many, (a) little, (a) few, other(s), another, none, one, either, neither 等。

由 body, one, thing 构成的合成代词如下：somebody, anybody, everybody, nobody; someone, anyone, everyone, no one; something, anything, everything, nothing。

一般来讲，修饰不定代词的词（不定代词的定语）要置于其后。

作用	示例
作主语	***Some*** are doctors, ***some*** are nurses. 有些人是医生，有些人是护士。 ***Someone*** has let the news out. 有人（某人）把这个消息泄露出去了。 ***All*** that glitters is not gold. 闪光的不一定都是金子。 ***Both*** of them are teachers. 他们两人都是教师。 ***Either*** of them will agree to this arrangement. 他们两人中会有（一个）人同意这样的安排。 ***Neither*** was satisfactory. 两个都不令人满意。 ***None*** of the problems is /are easy to solve. 这些问题没有一个是容易解决的。 ***Nobody*** knows his name. 没有人知道他的名字。 ***Everybody*** likes swimming. 每个人都喜欢游泳。 ***Everything*** is ready, isn't it? 一切都准备好了，对吗？ ***Anyone*** who comes first can get a ticket. 最先到的（任何）人可以得到一张票。 ***Others*** may object to this plan. 别人可能会反对这个计划。 ***Something*** goes wrong, doesn't it? （某方面）出问题了，是吗？ ***Much*** of the time was spent on learning. 大量时间都花在学习上。
作宾语	I know ***nothing*** about it. 这件事情我一点都不知道。 I don't know ***any*** of them. 他们，我（任何）一个也不认识。 To say ***something*** is one thing, to do is another thing. 说（某事）是一回事，做是另一回事。 You haven't called ***anyone/anybody*** up, have you? 你没给谁（任何人）打过电话，是吗？ —Do you have a car? —你有一辆小汽车吗？ —Yes, I have ***one***.—是的，我有一辆。 She said good-bye to ***everyone***. 她和每个人告别。 Are you going to buy ***anything***? 你会去买（一些）东西吗？
作表语	That's ***all*** I know. 这就是我知道的（全部）。 I'm not ***somebody***. I'm ***nobody***. 我不是重要人物，我是个无名小卒。（引申含义） That's ***nothing***. 那没有什么。
作定语	Do you have ***any*** books? 你有（任何）书吗？ I am going to get ***some*** ink. 我去弄点（一些）墨水。 Where are the ***other*** students? 其他学生去哪儿了？ She knows ***no*** English. 她根本就（一点也）不懂英语。 There is ***a little*** water in the pond. 池塘里还有一点水。 This watch doesn't work, I must get ***another*** one. 这块表坏了，我该买另一块了。 I go to school ***every*** day. 我每天去学校上学。 I have ***many*** books to give you. 我有许多书要给你。
定语后置	Can you tell ***something*** interesting? 你能讲些有趣的事情吗？（定语 interesting） Is there ***anybody*** important here? 这儿有大人物吗？（定语 important） Would you like ***something*** to eat? 要来些吃的东西吗？（定语 to eat） Isn't there ***something*** wrong with you? 难道你没问题吗？（定语 wrong with you）

4. 指示代词的用法

指示说明近处或者远处、上文或者下文、以前或者现在的人或事物。指示代词既可以单独使用做句子的主语、宾语或表语，也可以作定语修饰名词。

（1）指示代词的分类及含义。

单数	复数	含义
this（这个）	these（这些）	指代在时间上或空间上离说话人较近的人或物
that（那个）	those（那些）	指代在时间上或空间上离说话人较远的人或物 指代上文提过的词或句
such（这样的人或物）		指代上文提过的人和物
same（同样的人或物）		指代和上文提过的相同的人和物
it（这人或这物）		指代自然现象、时间、距离、身份不清的人或物 指代句子或句子的一部分

（2）指示代词的用法。

指示代词	作用
this / that these / those	You like *this* but I like *that*. 你喜欢这个，而我喜欢那个。（宾语） What is the use of *these* books？这些书的用途是什么？（定语） *This* is a boy and *those* are girls. 这是个男孩，那些是女孩。（主语） My point is *this*. 我的观点就是如此。（表语） He broke the window, and *that* cost him 10 dollars. 他打破了窗玻璃，那要花费他10美元。（主语，指代前句） The weather of Kunming is better than *that*（=the weather）of Beijing. 昆明的天气比北京好。（宾语，指代前词）
such /same	Remember never to do *such* things. 记得永远不要做这样的事情。（宾语） Do the *same* as the teacher tells you. 按老师说的做。（宾语） *Such* is my answer. 这就是我的答案。（表语倒装）
it	—Who is *it*? 是谁？ —*It*'s me! 是我！（主语，身份不清） *It*'s 3 o'clock in the afternoon. 现在是下午3点。（时间） *It*'s about 5 kilometres away. 大概有5千米远。（距离） *It*'s raining now. 现在正在下雨。（主语，自然现象） *It*'s important to learn English well. 学好英语很重要。（形式主语） You'll find *it* easy to make a kite. 你会发现制作风筝很简单。（形式宾语）

Part 4　Unit Practice

1. Read aloud the alphabet correctly.
2. Write down the letters which sound as follows.

   [æ]_____　　[k]_____　　[e]_____　　[dʒ]_____　　[ɑ]_____
   [kw]_____　　[I]_____　　[ks]_____　　[j][I]_____　　[ɒ]_____

3. Put the school languages into English.

   我们来点名。
   听到名字请回答"到"。
   今天星期几？
   我们来做律动吧！
   和着音乐用手打拍子。
   跟我一起做动作。

4. Put the following sentences into Chinese.

   （1）Children grow and develop through play.
   （2）Young children explore the world with their five senses.
   （3）Play time is more than toy time.
   （4）Types of play include object play, sensory motor play, social play and dramatic play.
   （5）Rotate props periodically to maintain and stimulate children's interest.

5. Read the words and name them.

   impossible_____　　　unpleasant_____　　　disorder_____
   minibus_____　　　　overwork_____　　　　pre-school_____
   kilogram_____　　　　nonstop_____　　　　mislead_____
   anti-war_____　　　　bilingual_____　　　　recall_____

6. Chose the best answer to complete the sentences.

   （1）Would you lend me _____ of your money, please?
   　　A. any　　　　B. many　　　　C. some　　　　D. a lot of
   （2）Sorry, but I have only _____ ink left over.
   　　A. little　　　B. few　　　　C. a little　　　D. a few
   （3）_____ who come from the countryside, please fill out the form.
   　　A. All　　　　B. Anyone　　　C. These　　　D. Those
   （4）She went for a swim in the pool yesterday and I'll do _____ this afternoon.
   　　A. it　　　　B. such　　　　C. same　　　　D. the same
   （5）There're tall buildings on _____ side of the street.
   　　A. either　　　B. both　　　　C. every　　　　D. any

(6) _____ must do _____ best to serve the people.
   A. One; his   B. One; her   C. One; one   D. Ones; ones'
(7) He has quite a lot of interesting magazines but I have _____ .
   A. no   B. none   C. no one   D. neither
(8) _____ are fond of collecting stamps.
   A. Both the children   B. Both of children
   C. My both children   D. Both of the my children
(9) Of the 4 books, one is written by a young writer and _____ by an old one.
   A. other three   B. three other   C. the other three   D. the three other
(10) He invited the three of _____ , Bob, Tom and _____ .
   A. we; me   B. us; I   C. we; I   D. us; me

Part 5 Extended Reading

Dramatic Play Center

Young children love make-believe activities. The Dramatic Play Center allows children the opportunity to act out their real world. They can experience different roles, express feelings, imitate actions and character traits of those around them. It is a place where the most creative, spontaneous and involved play occurs. The open-endedness of the dramatic play center allows each child to be successful on their own developmental level.

Child Development

The Dramatic Play Center offers many experiences to facilitate growth and enhance skills in all areas of development.

Physical Skills: develop fine motor skills, extend gross motor development, and develop visual discrimination and eye-hand coordination.

Social/Emotional Skills: provide a means to express feelings and emotions; develop awareness of self, family, and society; promote cooperation, working with others, sharing and taking turns.

Language Skills: increase oral communication skills, extend and enhance vocabulary, extend gross motor development, develop pretend reading and writing.

Intellectual Skills: develop creativity and imagination, promote problem-solving skills, and extend symbolic use of items and abstract thinking.

Points to Remember

• Arrange the Dramatic Play Center next to other noisy active areas.

• Create boundaries on three sides of the area to keep materials contained.

• Place only a few items in the Dramatic Play Center when introduced.

• Add additional items and props to enhance play and the current theme.

• Keep props clean and in good repair.

• Use labels and pictures to show where items belong to facilitate clean-up.

• Interact on the child's level by sitting or kneeling.

• Participate when invited and model the play. Encourage children to talk about what they are doing.

• Allow children to resolve conflicts independently.

• Provide small labeled boxes or baskets for small items and hooks or coat racks for clothes.

• Provide for literacy opportunities, such as books and writing materials.

Suggested Dramatic Play Center Materials

Cups	Living furniture
Dinnerware	Dress-up clothes
Table and chairs	Wallets
Kitchen items	Dolls and baby items
Vases and flowers	Toiletries
Empty food boxes	Old hair dryers without the cord
Broom and dustpan	Full-length mirror
Phone and phone book	Lunch boxes
Silverware	Child-safe tool belt, tools
Cookware	Magazines
Kitchen furniture	Suitcases
Aprons	Purses
Plastic food	Notepad and pencils
Dish towels	Multicultural clothing and materials
Belts, shoes	Cell phone

Prop Box Ideas

Provide dramatic play and prop box enrichments as opportunities to build upon skills and learn concepts.

The Beach
- Blanket
- Picnic basket
- Beach umbrella
- Sunglasses
- Beach ball
- Pretend suntan lotion
- Beach towel
- Buckets and shovels
- Shells
- Snorkels
- Fins
- Flip flops

Restaurant
- Tablecloth
- Napkins
- Tableware
- Menus made with food pictures
- Dishes
- Aprons
- Trays
- Play food
- Hats
- Sign for restaurant
- Order pads/pencils

Firefighter
- Yellow rubber raincoats
- Old vacuum hose
- Whistle
- Stepladder
- Phone
- Flashlight
- Boots
- Fire safety posters
- Gloves
- Baby dolls (to rescue)
- Walkie-talkies
- Fire hats

Post Office
- Envelopes
- Stamps (seals/stickers)
- Duffle bag
- Mailperson hat
- Cash register
- Old blue shirt
- Stickers
- Paper punch
- Postcards
- Scale
- Mailbox
- Pens
- Pencils
- Paper
- Junk mail
- Boxes
- Packages
- Checkbook
- Date book
- Play desk

Grocery Store
- Play food
- Egg cartons
- Check out area
- Play money
- Grocery cart or basket
- Aprons
- Paper bags
- Cash register or scanner
- Sale flyers
- Purses and wallets
- Plastic fruit/vegetables
- Coupons

Police Officer
- Pad for writing tickets
- Stop signs
- Small clipboard
- Police hat
- License plates
- Whistle (siren)
- Steering wheel
- Black belt
- 911 signs
- Blue shirt
- Walkie-talkie
- Badge

Bank
- Play money
- Bankbooks
- Adding machine/calculator
- Rubber stamps/ink pads
- Teller window
- Deposit slips/checks
- Cash box
- Paper/pens
- Coin rolls

- Magnifying glass
- Newspaper

Bakery
- Fresh play dough
- Rolling pins
- Aprons
- Oven mitts
- Cookie sheets
- Chef's hat
- Muffin tins
- Cake pans
- Cake decorations
- Order pads
- Measuring spoons
- Pictures of baked goods
- Mixing bowls
- Spoons
- Recipes
- Cookie cutters
- Flour shaker
- Cookbooks

Veterinarian
- Stuffed animals
- Gauze
- Surgical masks
- Pamphlets on animals
- Cotton balls
- Plastic gloves
- Play money
- Needle-less syringes
- Exam table
- Empty medicine bottles
- Pet brushes
- White lab coat
- Pet carriers
- Magnifying glass

UNIT 3

The Benefits of Playgrounds

> " Perhaps imagination is only intelligence having fun. "
>
> —George Scialabba

Learning Objectives

Students will
- ★ review vowel sounds
- ★ be familiar with school languages, chants, songs and stories
- ★ learn how to play a game for children
- ★ master new words and expressions
- ★ understand what play is and learn how to help children learn to negotiate, compromise, work together, and also to control themselves
- ★ review derivation words and numeral

Part 1 Skills for Pre-school English Teaching

Phonetics

English Phonics（Ⅱ） 自然拼读法（二）

Vowel Sounds 元音字母的读音

Vowel	Long		Short			
	Stressed		Stressed		Unstressed	
Aa	[eɪ] [ɑ:]	snake game after dance	[æ] [ɒ]	apple cat hand want what was	[ə] [ɪ]	allow breakfast village manager
Ee	[i:]	be me she we these theme	[e] [ɪ]	forget ten when pretty detail	[ə] [ɪ]	children parent before ticket
Ii (Yy)	[aɪ]	die nice ice bye my cry	[ɪ]	begin cylinder him is system	[ə] [ɪ]	university family animal bicycle lady
Oo	[əu] [u:]	go home open move prove	[ɒ] [ʌ]	dog stop on come mother	[ə]	bottom welcome somebody today
Uu	[ju:] [u:]	excuse unit blue June rule true	[ʌ] [ɪ] [u]	bus under busy business put sugar	[ə] [ju] [u]	succeed difficult popular January wonderful useful
Ee	Silent	age apple bike come due face leave theme tie use				

School Languages

Outdoor Activities 户外活动

- It's time for / to do morning exercises.
  该做早操了！
- Let' go out. / Let's go out to play, shall we?
  我们出去吧。/ 我们出去玩吧，好吗？
- Line up, please./ Make one line / two lines. Hurry up.
  请排好队。/ 站一排／两排。快一点！
- Boys a line, girls a line. Boys line up here. Girls line up there.
  男生一排，女生一排。男生站这边。女生站那边。

- One by one, please./ No pushing. /No cutting in./Watch your steps.
  一个一个走。/ 不要推搡。/ 不许插队。/ 注意脚下！
- At ease. Attention. Stand straight.
  稍息！立正！站直！
- Let's count off. One, two, three...
  我们来报数。一、二、三……
- Quick time, march. / Mark time, left, right, left, right...
  齐步走！/ 原地踏步走！左、右、左、右……
- Turn left/ right. Halt. Arms out. Arms in.
  左转弯！/ 右转弯！立定！伸臂！收臂！
- Eyes right/front. Now let's go back.
  向右看齐！/ 向前看！回教室！
- Go ahead./Keep going./Get a move on.
  向前走。/ 一直走。/ 赶快。

Chants & Songs

Five Little Monkeys

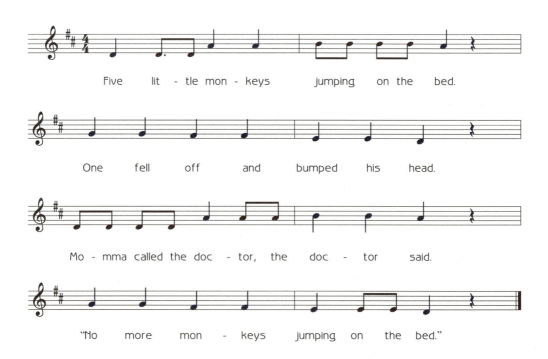

Five little monkeys jumping on the bed.
One fell off and bumped his head.
Momma called the doctor, the doctor said.
"No more monkeys jumping on the bed."

Five Little Monkeys 五只小猴

Five little monkeys jumping on the bed
One fell off and bumped his head
So Momma called the doctor and the doctor said
No more monkeys jumping on the bed!

Four little monkeys jumping on the bed
One fell off and bumped his head
So Momma called the doctor and the doctor said
No more monkeys jumping on the bed!

FIVE LITTLE MONKEYS

Three little monkeys jumping on the bed
One fell off and bumped his head
So Momma called the doctor and the doctor said
No more monkeys jumping on the bed!

Two little monkeys jumping on the bed
One fell off and bumped his head
So Momma called the doctor and the doctor said
No more monkeys jumping on the bed!

One little monkey jumping on the bed
He fell off and bumped his head
So Momma called the doctor and the doctor said
No more monkeys jumping on the bed!

No little monkeys jumping on the bed
None fell off and bumped his head
So Momma called the doctor and the doctor said
Put those monkeys back in bed!

Stories

My Birthday Story 我生日的故事

My birthday is coming up. I want to have a birthday party.
I want to invite my friends. All my friends are coming to the party.
There are lots of balloons in the room. I pop the balloons by mistake.
There are lots of presents in the room. I want to open them.
I open one, and it is a cute little tea cup.
I drop it, and break it by mistake.
For lunch, I eat spaghetti. I spill the sauce by mistake.
I drink orange juice. I spill it on my friend by mistake.
Finally, the birthday cake comes out.
I want to blow out the candles. I burn my forehead by mistake.
I want to cut the cake. I drop the knife by mistake.
I popped the balloons, broke the tea cup, spilled the spaghetti sauce and orange juice, burnt my forehead, and dropped the knife.
But that is okay, because today is my birthday.

Game

Matching by Touching 五体投地

Objective: Listening and reacting

Teaching aid: flash cards; a timer

Steps：1. Scatter the flash cards over the floor.

   2. The child touches the cards with parts of the body following the teacher's instructions "Put your head on... " "Put your hip on... " "Put your left hand on... " "Put your knee on... "

Tips：1. Make sure that the cards are not too scattered, so that the children can see and reach them easily.

   2. The flash cards can be of pictures, alphabet, numbers or words.

Extension: Team work.

   1. Form 2 teams and 1 kid at a time from each team to compete.

   2. Set 2 sets of flash cards scattered over the floor for the 2 teams.

   3. The teacher says one of the words from the cards, the competitors quickly touches it using any part of their bodies, and once touch, keep still till the end of the game. Then the teacher says another word, the kids use their other parts to quickly touch the right card. The kid with more cards touched correctly in a certain time scores, and then other team members take turns to come to compete. The team scoring more wins.

 Part 2   Pre-school Education in English

The benefits of Playgrounds for Children Aged 0-5

Playgrounds provide crucial and vital opportunities for children to play. There is a substantial number of researches showing a clear link between play and brain development, motor skills and social capabilities.

All learning—emotional, social, motor and cognitive—is accelerated, facilitated, and fueled by the pleasure of play. Playgrounds that promote different types of play are vital for a child's cognitive, emotional, physical, and social development. The more specific ways in which playgrounds and play equipment, similar to those being installed in Shasta County, promote growth are described as below.

Play and Free Play

What is play? Play is simply having fun, the spontaneous activity of children. Play encompasses many things. It can be done with the body (running, jumping, dancing), the mind (fantasy play), props (building blocks, pushing a toy) and words (jokes, singing). Play is fueled and driven by curiosity. Play begins simple and grows more complex as the child grows.

Playgrounds provide an opportunity for free play. Free play differs from the structured play of recess or organized sports and games. Playground free play allows children to play any way they choose, supported by a wide range of structures and spaces. Free play allows the children to explore according to their natural tendencies, and allows them to learn from one another and to interact with a wide range of age groups.

Language Development, Intelligence, and Social Skills

Play is the primary vehicle for development of the imagination, intelligence, and language. The playground maximizes opportunities to engage in a greater amount of play with their peers. The interaction with their peers allows children to express ideas and feelings and develop oral skills. Play structures promote social play because they provide children with places to congregate and communicate. Through the act of playing, they learn social and cultural rules, and experiment with various emotions, and explore the socially shared system of symbols. By playing they also learn by physical and mental trial-and-error, through interaction with their environment and peers, the ability to discriminate between relevant and irrelevant information. Simply put, a shortage of playgrounds can add to children's passivity.

An example of how free play in playgrounds aids the development of social skills can be seen in the spontaneous creation of "games." Whether it be a game of tag or fantasy play that makes a playground structure into castle with the children, assigning themselves specific roles (guard, king, queen, etc.), peer interaction is required to establish the "rules of the game" and play begins. Children learn to negotiate, compromise, work together, and also control themselves and tolerate their frustrations in a social setting, because without abiding by the invented "rules" children cannot continue to play successfully with their peers. The modular structures that link different playground elements together provide opportunities for socialization by providing different kinds of interaction—nooks for single children; retreats for two or three; places for one on one adult/child interactions; and places for small groups.

Notes

1. Background

The Shasta Children and Families First Commission (SCFFC) has funded several projects which in part or whole create playgrounds for young children aged 0-5. Each of these playgrounds will be developed separately with local community input, but share several fundamental characteristics. Each will be created in a safe, fenced area and will contain various play equipment which meets state safety standards, all specifically designed for very young children. The Commission is interested in how these playgrounds will impact the healthy development of these children.

沙斯塔儿童和家庭第一委员会(SCFFC)资助了几个项目，这些项目部分或全部为 0~5 岁的儿童创造了游乐场地。每一个游乐场都将由当地社区投入并独立开发，但也有一些共同的基本特征。每一个都将在一个安全的、有围栏的区域内创建，并将包含各种符合国家安全标准的游戏设备，这些设备都是专门为低龄儿童设计的。委员会感兴趣的是这些游乐场将如何对这些儿童的健康发展产生影响。

Shasta County, officially the County of Shasta, is a county in the northern portion of California in the U.S.A. 沙斯塔县是美国加利福尼亚州北部的一个县。

2. All learning—emotional, social, motor and cognitive—is accelerated, facilitated, and fueled by the pleasure of play.

所有的学习（不管是情绪上、社交上、运动上还是认知上）都是由玩耍的乐趣来加速、促进和推动的。

3. The more specific ways in which playgrounds and play equipment, similar to those being installed in Shasta County, promote growth are described below.

与在沙斯塔县安装方法类似，促进成长的游乐场和游戏设备更具体的方法描述如下。

Syntactic analysis：主语（The... ways）+ 定语从句（in which... growth）+ 谓语（被动语态 are described below）

in which... promote growth 是定语从句, similar to those being installed in Shasta County 是定语从句中的插入语，作状语；定语从句结构：

主语（playgrounds and play equipment）+ 插入语 + 谓宾（promote growth）

4. Free play differs from the structured play of recess or organized sports and games.

自由玩耍不同于有条理的课间休息玩耍或有组织的运动和比赛。

differ from 与……不同；区别于……

e.g. That arrangement differs from the one I had in mind. 那种安排同我原先所想的不同。

5. Play structures promote social play because they provide children with places to congregate and communicate. 游乐设施促进了社交游戏的发展，因为它们为儿童提供了聚集和交流的场所。

provide... with... 给……提供；以……装备

e.g. They provide us with food. 他们供给我们食物。

6. Through the act of playing they learn social and cultural rules, and experiment with various emotions, and explore the socially shared system of symbols.

通过玩耍的行为，他们可以学会社交和文化的规则，体验各种各样的情绪，并探索社会共享的符号系统。

experiment with 进行试验；体验；试用；以……做试验

e.g. He believes that students should be encouraged to experiment with bold ideas. 他认为应该鼓励学生们将大胆的想法付诸试验。

system of symbols 符号系统：符号主义起源于信息加工理论，该理论认为语言就是一个符号系统。

7. By playing they also learn by physical and mental trial-and-error, through interaction with their environment and peers, the ability to discriminate between relevant and irrelevant information.

通过玩耍，他们也可以经过身心反复试错、与环境和同伴的互动，来学会区分相关信息和不相关信息的能力。

trial-and-error【心理学】尝试—错误，（为求完善的）反复试验，试错法

e.g. We need to learn from doing, by trial-and-error. 我们需要通过尝试和犯错，从实践中学习。

8. Simply put, a shortage of playgrounds can add to children's passivity.

简而言之，游乐场的缺乏会增加儿童的被动性。

simply put 简言之；简单地说

e.g. Simply put, you are the one who is going to educate yourself.

简单地说，你将是一个自己教育自己的人。

9. Whether it be a game of tag or fantasy play that makes a playground structure into castle with the children assigning themselves specific roles (guard, king, queen, etc.), peer interaction is required to establish the "rules of the game" and play begins.

无论是捉人游戏，抑或是将游乐设施做成城堡，让儿童来自己分配角色（守卫、国王、皇后等）的幻想游戏，都需要同伴的互动来建立"游戏规则"并开始游戏。

Syntactic analysis：这是一个复杂的复合句。主句是 peer interaction is required... and play begins. 而 Whether... or... 引导包含选择范围的让步状语从句，意为"不管……"。让步状语从句中又包含一个定语从句 that makes... etc. 修饰先行词 fantasy play 。

Whether it be... 让步状语从句谓语用动词原型主要用于书面的正式语体，有虚拟语气条件句的意味。非正式语体可使用陈述语气。

a game of tag 捉人游戏，就是大家跑，一个人追。

with the children assigning... 复合结构（介词＋宾语＋宾补）做伴随性状语，意为"同时儿童在分配……"

e.g. He soon fell asleep with the light still burning. 灯还亮着，他很快就睡着了。

10. The modular structures that link different playground elements together provide opportunities for socialization by providing different kinds of interaction—nooks for single children; retreats for two or three; places for one on one adult/child interactions; and places for small groups.

将不同的游乐场元素连接在一起的模块化结构通过配备不同类型的互动来提供社会化的机会——独自一人的角落；两三个孩子的僻静处；成人、儿童一对一互动的场所和小群体的场所。

Useful Words & Expressions

crucial [ˈkru:ʃəl] *adj.* 重要的；决定性的

vital [ˈvaɪtl] *adj.* 至关重要的；有活力的

substantial [səbˈstænʃəl] *adj.* 实质的；内容充实的
　　　　　　　　　　　n. 本质；重要材料

accelerate [əkˈseləreɪt] *vt.* 促进；（使）加快
　　　　　　　　　　　vi. 加快，加速

facilitate [fəˈsɪlɪteɪt] *vt.* 帮助；促进，助长

fuel [ˈfjuːəl] *n.* 燃料；食物
　　　　　　vt. 给……加燃料，给……加油；激起
　　　　　　vi. 补充燃料

encompass [ɪnˈkʌmpəs; en-] *vt.* 包含；包围；环绕

fantasy play 幻想游戏；幻象游戏

complex [ˈkɒmpleks] *adj.* 复杂的；合成的
　　　　　　　　　　n. 复合体；综合设施

recess [rɪˈses] *n.* 休息；隐蔽处
　　　　　　　vt. （暂时）休会，休课，休庭
　　　　　　　vi. 休息，休会，休庭

tendency [ˈtendənsi] *n.* 倾向，趋势；癖好
　　natural tendency 自然倾向，本能，本性

vehicle [ˈviːəkl] *n.* 车辆，交通工具；媒介物

maximize [ˈmæksɪmaɪz] *vt.* 最大化，极为重视

peer [pɪə] *n.* 贵族；同辈，同等的人；同伴，伙伴

adj. 贵族的；（年龄、地位等）同等的
congregate [ˈkɒŋgrɪgeɪt] *vt.& vi.* 使集合，聚集
adj. 聚集的，集合的
error [ˈerə] *n.* 误差；错误；过失
discriminate [dɪˈskrɪmɪneɪt] *vt.* 歧视；区别；辨别
vi. 区别；辨别
relevant [ˈreləvənt] *adj.* 相关的；有意义的
irrelevant [ɪˈrelɪvənt] *adj.* 不相干的；不切题的
shortage [ˈʃɔːtɪdʒ] *n.* 缺乏，缺少；不足
passivity [pæˈsɪvɪti] *n.* 被动性；被动结构；无抵抗
aid [eɪd] *n.* 帮助；助手；外援；辅助设备
vt.& vi. 帮助；救助；资助；促进
tag [tæg] *vt.* 附加；加标签于；起诉；紧跟

n. 标签；附属物；口头禅；称呼
assign [əˈsaɪn] *vt.* 分配；指派
compromise [ˈkɒmprəmaɪz] *vt.& vi.* 妥协；危害
n. 妥协，和解；折中
tolerate [ˈtɒləreɪt] *vt.* 忍受；默许；宽恕
frustration [frʌˈstreɪʃn] *n.* 挫折
modular [ˈmɒdjələ] *adj.* 模块化的；组合式的
socialization [ˌsəʊʃəlaɪˈzeɪʃn] *n.* 社会化；公有化
nook [nʊk] *n.* 角落；隐蔽处
retreat [rɪˈtriːt] *vi.* 撤退，后退；撤销
n. 撤回；僻静处，静居处
one on one（face to face）一对一

Ideological and Political Concept

　　游戏和玩耍是想象力、智力和语言发展的主要途径。通过游戏和玩耍的行为，幼儿可以学会社交和文化的规则，体验各种各样的情绪，并探索社会共享的符号系统。通过玩耍，幼儿也可以经过身心反复试错、与环境和同伴的互动来分辨是非真假。幼儿在社交环境中学习协商、妥协、共同合作，并且控制自己，容忍挫折，从而学会遵守规则。幼教工作者要以正确的价值观及情感态度在教育活动过程中给幼儿潜移默化的正面影响。

Part 3　English Proficiency

Word Building Ⅲ 构词（三）

Derivation Ⅱ 派生法（二）
Suffix—后缀

　　加后缀通常会改变单词的词类，构成意义相近的其他词性的词；少数后缀还会改变词义，变为与原来词义相反的新词。

Nouns & Verbs 名词和动词

Part of Speech		Suffix	Meaning	Examples
n. → n.		-eer	skilled in；engaged in 对……熟练；从事……	mountaineer 登山者；engineer 工程师；profiteer 投机者，奸商
		-ful	The amount or number that will fill 数量上的满	mouthful 满嘴；basketful 满篮；spoonful 满勺；handful 满手
		-ship	status；condition 地位；身份；条件	fellowship 奖学金；relationship 关系；membership 会员资格
adj. → n.		-dom	domain; realm; condition 领域；环境；身份	freedom 自由；wisdom 智慧；boredom 无聊；officialdom 官僚作风
		-ity	abstract noun 构成抽象名词	falsity 不诚实；rapidity 迅速；actuality 现实；regularity 规律性
		-ness		carelessness 粗心；happiness 幸福；selfishness 自私；unexpectedness 意外
v. → n.		-al	the action or the result of 动作或结果	arrival 抵达；refusal 拒绝；signal 信号；removal 移动；survival 残存
		-ant	agent 施动者	inhabitant 居住者；contestant 竞争者；participant 参与者；lubricant 润滑油
		-ee	one who is the object of the verb 受动者	absentee（缺席者）；refugee（逃难者）；employee（雇员）；nominee（被提名者）
		-er/or	agent 施动者	creator 创造者；survivor 幸存者；driver 司机；New Yorker 纽约人
		-age	action of; instance of 作用，实例	coverage 所包括的范围；drainage 排水法；shrinkage 缩水
		-tion/ation	the process or state of，the product of 状态，产物	protection 保护；completion 完成；examination 考试；consideration 考虑
		-ment	the result of 结果	arrangement 安排；amazement 惊异
Verb 动词	n. → v.	-ate		hyphenate 以连字符连接
	adj. → v.	-en		sadden 使悲伤；quicken 使快速
	adj. → v. n. → v.	-ify		simplify 使简单；beautify 使美丽；identify 辨认；electrify 使通电
	adj. → v. n. → v.	-ize		modernize 使现代化；civilize 使文明；symbolize 用符号表现

Numeral 数词

表示数目多少或顺序先后的词叫数词，数词分为基数词和序数词。数词在句中可以作主语、宾语、表语、定语和同位语等成分。

1. 掌握基数词的构成及基本用法：基数词表示数字或数量多少

（1）基数词的构成。

1 one	11 eleven	21 twenty-one	40 forty	10,000 ten thousand
2 two	12 twelve	22 twenty-two	50 fifty	100,000 a hundred thousand
3 three	13 thirteen	23 twenty-three	60 sixty	1,000,000 a million
4 four	14 fourteen	24 twenty-four	70 seventy	10,000,000 ten million
5 five	15 fifteen	25 twenty-five	80 eight	100,000,000 a hundred million
6 six	16 sixteen	26 twenty-six	90 ninety	1,000,000,000 a billion
7 even	17 seventeen	27 twenty-seven	100 a hundred	101 a hundred and one
8 eight	18 eighteen	28 twenty-eight	1,000 a thousand	210 two hundred and ten
9 nine	19 nineteen	29 twenty-nine	815 eight hundred and fifteen	
10 ten	20 twenty	30 thirty	9,999 nine thousand nine hundred and ninety-nine	

（2）基数词的语法作用。

Three will be fine. 三个就行了。（主语）

Three and five is ***eight***. 3+5=8 （表语）

—How many do you want? 你要多少?

—I want ***twenty***. 我要 20 个。（宾语）

Four hundred years ago, the number was over ***500 million***. 四百年前数量是 5 亿。（定语；宾语）

We ***five*** went to the park yesterday. 我们 5 个人昨天去公园了。（同位语）

（3）基数词不表示确定数目或数量。

Thousands of people attended the funeral. 数千人参加了葬礼。

He went to the United States in his twenties. 他二十几岁时就去了美国。

They arrived in ***twos and threes***.　他们三三两两地到达了。

I'm all ***at sixes and sevens***. 我这儿什么都是乱七八糟的。

We have seen this play before ***in the 1990s***. 我们在 20 世纪 90 年代曾看过这个剧。

He's starred in ***dozens of*** films. 他主演过几十部影片。

He had mentored ***scores of*** younger doctors. 他指导过许多更年轻的医生。

2. 掌握序数词的构成及基本用法：序数词表示顺序和等级

（1）序数词的构成。

first	1st	seventh	7th	thirteenth	13rd	nineteenth	19th
second	2nd	eighth	8th	fourteenth	14th	twentieth	20th
third	3rd	ninth	9th	fifteenth	15th	twenty-first	21st
fourth	4th	tenth	10th	sixteenth	16th	twenty-second	22nd
fifth	5th	eleventh	11th	seventeenth	17th	twenty-third	23rd
sixth	6th	twelfth	12nd	eighteenth	18th	twenty-fourth	24th

续表

twenty-fifth	25th	twenty-ninth	29th	sixtieth	60th	hundredth	100th
twenty-sixth	26th	thirtieth	30th	seventieth	70th	thousandth	1,000th
twenty-seventh	27th	fortieth	40th	eightieth	80th	millionth	100,000th
twenty-eighth	28th	fiftieth	50th	ninetieth	90th	billionth	100,000,000th

（2）序数词的语法作用：序数词表顺序，主要作定语，其前面须加上定冠词 the；此外，也作主语、宾语、表语和同位语等。

The third is bigger than *the second*. 第三个比第二个大。（主语；宾语）

He was among *the first* to arrive. 他是首批到达的人员之一。（宾语）

She's often *the first* to go to school. 她经常第一个去上学。（表语）

May is *the fifth* month of the year. 五月是一年中的第 5 个月。（定语）

Who is the woman, *the second* in the line? 排中第二位的那个女的是谁？（同位语）

（3）日常交际用语中用基数词代替序数词表达编号顺序，基数词后置。

the second part = Part Two　第二部分

the first chapter = Chapter One　第一章

the fourth section = Section Four　第四节

the twelfth lesson = Lesson Twelve　第十二课

Page 32　第 32 页

Room 305　第 305 房间

Bus No.12　第 12 路公交车

The No.2 Middle School 第二中学

（4）序数词前不加定冠词 the 的情况。

前有修饰语	Mother was *my first* teacher in my life. 妈妈是我生命中的第一个老师。 Tom is *Lily's third* boyfriend. 汤姆是莉莉的第 3 个男朋友。
前有 a /an 表 "又一 / 再一"	Please give me *a second* chance. 请再给我一次机会。 The poor woman had *a third* baby. 那个可怜的女人又生了第三个宝宝。
作状语	Who got there *second*? 谁第二个到那儿的？ I finished the work *first*. 我最先完成那项工作。
分数	*One fifth of* the students here are from the country. 这儿 1/5 的学生来自农村。 *Three fourths* of the students here are from the country. 这里 3/4 的学生来自农村。

3. 掌握年、月、日的表达法及数字的表达法：英式英语和美式英语中对年月日的表达大有不同。日期的定冠词不一定写出来，但要读出来。

英式：29(th) /Twenty-ninth March, 2017; 29. 03. 2017; 29 / 03 /2017

读作 the twenty-ninth of March, twenty seventeen /two thousand and seventeen

美式：March 29(th) / twenty-ninth, 2017; 03. 29. 2017; 03 /29 /2017

读作 March the twenty-ninth, twenty seventeen /two thousand and seventeen

Part 4 Unit Practice

1. Read aloud and write down the following words according to the phonics.

   snake / hand / village / theme / forget / ticket / bye / system / animal / prove

   [wɔnt] _____   [truː] _____   [ˈbɪzi] _____

   [aɪs] _____   [ˈpriti] _____   [ˈjuːnɪt] _____

2. Put the school languages into English.

   排队！站成一排！   齐步走！向左转！向右转！
   不要推搡，小心脚下！   向前看齐！手放下！
   站直！稍息！立正！报数！   向前走，不要停！

3. Put the following phrases and sentences into Chinese.

   (1) Playgrounds provide crucial and vital opportunities for children to play.
   (2) Play is the primary vehicle for development of the imagination, intelligence, and language.
   (3) Children learn to negotiate, compromise, work together, and also to control themselves.
   (4) the structured play of recess or organized sports and games
   (5) Play begins simple and grows more complex as the child grows.

4. Read the derived words and name them.

   bore**dom** _____   hand**ful** _____   member**ship** _____
   examina**tion** _____   care**less** _____   regulari**ty** _____
   selfish**ness** _____   remov**al** _____   employ**ee** _____

5. Chose the best answer to complete the sentences.

   (1) —What would you like, sir?
       — _____ .
       A. Two pop   B. Two bottles pop
       C. Two bottles of pop   D. Two bottle of pop

   (2) _____ girls took part in the Happy Girl Competition but only a few of them could succeed.
       A. Million of   B. Many million of
       C. One million of   D. Millions of

   (3) _____ of the earth _____ covered by sea.
       A. Three fourth; is   B. Three fourths; is
       C. Three fourth; are   D. Three fourths; are

   (4) I got a beautiful bike on _____ birthday. I liked it very much.
       A. fifteenth   B. fifteen   C. my fifteen   D. my fifteenth

   (5) —Do you know the boy _____ is sitting next to Peter?
       —Yes. He is Peter's friend. They are celebrating his _____ birthday.
       A. /; ninth   B. that; ninth   C. who; ninth   D. who; the ninth

（6）I got a good present on my _____ birthday.

　　A. nine　　　　B. ninth　　　　C. the nine　　　　D. the ninth

（7）—Have you seen the CCTV news on TV?

　　—Yes, _____ children had a good festival on the _____ Children's Day.

　　A. millions of; sixty　　　　B. ten millions; sixtieth

　　C. millions of; sixtieth　　　D. ten millions; sixty

（8）_____ trees have been planted near here, so the air is very fresh.

　　A. Two hundreds　　　　B. Hundred of

　　C. Hundreds of　　　　　D. Hundreds

（9）_____ of the land in that district _____ covered with trees and grass.

　　A. Two fifths; is　　　　B. Two fifth; are

　　C. Two fifth; is　　　　 D. Two fifths; are

（10）Although I failed four times, my father encouraged me to have a _____ try.

　　A. third　　　B. fourth　　　C. fifth　　　D. sixth

Part 5　Extended Reading

Math Center

It is easy to get students involved with numbers, measuring and problem-solving when the Math Center is equipped with a wide variety of concrete materials. This provides a solid foundation for exploring math concepts, practicing new skills and applying skills they have mastered.

Child Development

The Math Center offers many experiences to facilitate growth and enhance skills in all areas of development.

Physical Skills: strengthen fine motor control, and refine eye-hand coordination.

Social/Emotional Skills: develop self-control, promote perseverance and confidence, enhance cooperation through sharing materials and working together to solve a problem.

Language Skills: introduce the language of mathematics and enhance the ability to ask questions and explain solutions.

Intellectual Skills: introduce and refine sorting, matching, classifying, sequencing, patterning, one-to-one correspondence, rote counting, number combinations, problem solving.

Points to Remember

• Introduce new math materials one at a time.

• Model appropriate use, care, and clean-up procedures.

• Let students freely explore the materials before asking them to do a specific task.

• Have students use a variety of math materials to work on the same skill or concept.

• Search out math materials that are fun and unusual.

• Make math meaningful. Examples: making change for a store, measuring for cooking, dividing snacks into equal shares, or graphing choices for a class field trip.

• Provide a variety of ways for students to record what they have done in the Math Center: drawing, charts, graphs, books, rubber stamps, stickers or real objects.

• Observe and listen to students as they work in the center. This will give an insight into their emerging concept of number.

• Extend student activities by introducing mathematical languages during their play.

Suggested Math Center Materials

Collectible manipulatives: buttons, keys, colored pasta, shells, rocks, bread tags, colored paper clips, beans, toothpicks

- Plastic counters
- Pattern blocks
- Pattern cards
- 1" colored cubes
- 1" wooden cubes
- Color tiles
- Attribute blocks
- Multilink cubes
- Parquetry blocks
- Sorting trays/bowls
- Measuring instruments such as rulers, yardsticks, measuring cups, measuring spoons
- Balance scales and things to weigh
- Pegboards and pegs
- Stringing beads
- Games and puzzles
- Dice and spinners
- Floor graph
- Magnetic board
- Magnetic shapes and numbers
- Individual marker boards and chalkboards
- Clock
- Play money
- Rubber stamps
- Math-related books, songs, poems, charts or posters
- Timers
- Dominoes
- Calendar
- Keys
- Beads
- Nuts, bolts, washers or screws
- Ice cube trays
- Shape templates and writing supplies
- Spools
- Clothespins
- Straws
- Number stencils
- Number stamps and pads
- Number lines
- Calculators
- Sorting containers
- Jars
- Cans
- Tubs

Zipper seal bags
Stickers
Playing cards
Adding machine tape for creating patterns
Cash register
Price tags
Coupons
Math big books
Counting charts
Color word charts

Shape charts
Games
Hula hoops for defining spaces
Egg cartons
Notebooks
Placemats
Trays
Lunch bags or gift sacks
Bulletin board

UNIT 4

Learning Environment I

> " Child development is '... a process of change in which a child learns to handle even more complex levels of moving, thinking, feeling and relating to others.' "
>
> —Mayers

Learning Objectives

Students will
- ★ review vowel digraph sounds
- ★ be familiar with school languages, chants, songs and stories
- ★ learn how to play a game for children
- ★ master new words and expressions
- ★ understand the learning environment is an important and powerful teaching tool and learn how to create a positive early childhood environment
- ★ review derivation words, adjectives and adverbs

Part 1 Skills for Pre-school English Teaching

Phonetics

English Phonics Ⅲ 自然拼读法（三）

Vowel Digraph Sounds（Part 1）元音字母组合的读音⑺

Vowel Digraph	Sounds & Examples				
	Long Vowel			Short Vowel	
Aa	ai ay	[eɪ]	paint rain train wait day play may say stay	[ɪ] [e] Silent	bargain captain Wednesday again against said certain curtain mountain
	au	[ɔ:] [ɑ:]	August autumn caught aunt laugh laughter	[ɒ]	Australia because
	aw	[ɔ:]	awful draw law strawberry		
Ee	ee ea	[i:] [eɪ] [ɪə]	been three sheep see eat read season speak break great steak idea real realize theatre	[e]	breakfast bread head heavy pleasure sweater
	ei ey	[i:] [eɪ] [aɪ]	ceiling receive seize grey hey obey they either neither height	[ɪ]	journey money monkey
	ew	[ju:] [u:]	new dew few sew dew drew crew Jew grew		

School Languages

Circle Time 圆圈时间

- Everybody, please take a seat in a circle.
  大家坐成圆圈。
- Quickly find your spot.
  快点找到自己的位置。
- Who's sitting in the wrong seat?
  谁做错了位置？

- Mary and Tom, please switch your seats.
  玛丽和汤姆换位置。
- Come and sit next to me.
  过来坐在我旁边。
- May I have your attention?
  大家请注意。
- Everybody's looking. Look here.
  看这里。
- Let's play silence game. No talking.
  我们来做沉默游戏。不要讲话。
- I need everyone to sit properly.
  我想要每个人都坐好。
- Put your hands on your knees.
  把手放在膝盖上。
- No playing during circle time. Behave yourself.
  圆圈时间不要玩耍。要守规矩。
- I like the way that Jerry is sitting.
  我喜欢杰瑞的坐姿。
- Are you going to listen?
  你们会听我说吗?
- Please go back to your seat.
  请回到你的座位上。
- I'm waiting for Isabel's going back to the circle.
  我在等待伊莎贝尔回到圆圈。

 **Chants & Songs**

Clap Your Hands 小手拍拍

Clap, clap, clap your hands as slowly as you can.
Clap, clap, clap your hands as quickly as you can.
Shake, shake, shake your hands as slowly as you can.
Shake, shake, shake your hands as quickly as you can.
Roll, roll, roll your hands as slowly as you can.
Roll, roll, roll your hands as quickly as you can.
Wiggle, wiggle, wiggle your fingers as slowly as you can.
Wiggle, wiggle, wiggle your fingers as quickly as you can.
Pound, pound, pound your fists as slowly as you can.
Pound, pound, pound your fists as quickly as you can.

Clap Your Hands

Clap your hands　　Touch your toes　　Turn a-round and　Put your fingers on your nose

Flap your arms　　Jump up high　　Wig-gle your fin-gers reach for the sky

The Hockey Pockey

THE HOCKEY POCKEY

You put your right foot　in - You take your right foot out　You put your

right foot in - and you shake it all a-bout　You do the ho-ckey po-ckey and you

turn your self a-round　That's what it's all a - bout

2. right hand
3. right shoulder
4. right hip
5. Wholeself

(替换歌词中的 right foot)

Stories

A Young Girl Knows How 小女孩能做到

She is six years old. She knows how to walk. She knows how to run. She knows how to swim. She knows how to play soccer. She knows how to ride a horse. She knows how to walk her dog. She knows how to read. She knows how to write.

Is That You？是你吗？

Today is mommy's birthday.
I have a special present for mommy. But I can't find her.
BOW WOW. "Is that you, mommy?"
No, it is a dog. Dogs say bow wow...
MEOW MEOW. "Is that you, mommy?"
No, it is a cat. Cats say meow meow...
MOO MOO. "Is that you, mommy?"
No, it is a cow. Cows say moo moo...
BAA BAA. "Is that you, mommy?"
No, it is a sheep. Sheep say baa baa...
CLUCK CLUCK. "Is that you, mommy?"
No, it is a chicken. Chickens say cluck cluck...
QUACK QUACK. "Is that you, mommy?"
No, it is a duck. Ducks say quack quack...
Oh, I hear something.
OINK OINK. "Is that you, mommy?"
Yes, it is. My mommy is here!

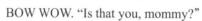

Wheel of Fortune 幸运轮盘

Objective: Identifying the color

Teaching aid: a spin with some pictures of different colors

Rules：1. Show the spin with pictures.

2. Mark each color 1 to 3 points in different grades.

3. Children take turns to spin the wheel. It rotates for a while and then it stops at one picture, the child must tell the name of the color based on that picture.

Tips: This is a very easy way to get students speaking. Use this spin with some pictures to make it even more specific. You may change the pictures according to whatever you want the children to practice.

Extension: Team work.

A child from each pair/team spins the wheel and when it stops at one picture, the child must ask a question based on that picture and the partner must answer it.

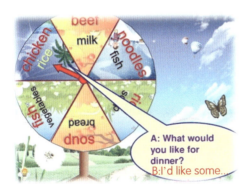

Part 2 Pre-school Education in English

The Early Childhood Learning Environment

The learning environment is an important and powerful teaching tool. Much of the early childhood teacher's work is done before the children ever arrive. If the environment is set up with the knowledge of how children learn and develop, it can positively support teaching and learning. A teacher experiencing difficulty with student behaviors should carefully evaluate the daily schedule, classroom arrangement, materials within each learning center, and the curriculum.

Best Practices

When creating a positive early childhood environment, the following practices should be observed:

- The classroom should be organized to foster exploration with learning materials.
- Learning materials should be concrete and relevant to a child's own life experiences (open-ended but purposeful).
- The classroom environment should be set up for choices.
- Learning experiences should be planned so teacher-initiated or child-initiated opportunities exist in small group contexts for acquiring new skills.
- Schedules should reflect active and quiet learning activities; large group, small group and individual learning time; teacher-directed and child-initiated activities; and indoor and outdoor activities.

The Daily Schedule

A daily schedule is essential to the basic structure of each day. Consistency enables children to feel secure, giving them the confidence and freedom to explore the environment. Although consistency is important, it is also necessary to remain flexible. Extra time may be needed if children are particularly interested in an activity or topic of discussion.

At the beginning of the year, shorter blocks of time are planned for large and small group activities. As the year progresses, learning center time will encompass a smaller portion of the day. Large group activities become fewer in number and often longer in length. Sample classroom schedules are available on the Early Childhood/Family Education Web site at <http://sde.state.ok.us> under the "helpful forms" link.

A Well-planned Schedule Will:

- Prioritize the need for children to interact with their peers, teachers and learning materials.
- Allow sufficient time for children to initiate and complete activities, and participate in creative movement and self-expression.
- Alternate active and less active learning moments rather than lengthy periods of sitting still.
- Respect the need for young children to rest or be active as is appropriate and does not compromise quality learning time.
- Reflect integrated teaching rather than class time separated subject by subject.
- Provide ample time for children to learn through center-based instruction.
- Allow for smooth transitions between activities or classrooms, with the teacher capitalizing on these transitions as learning moments.
- Provide opportunities for children to share with the group and take pride in their accomplishments.
- Structure time for collaborative planning so that children can develop their ownership with classroom learning activities.

Transitions

Transition is the process of moving from one activity to another. This is often difficult for young children. The teacher must prepare and prompt children for the change. Teachers use "attention getters" such as songs, signals, finger plays, rhymes, games and puppets to signal the change. Teachers who use transition activities will have calm, organized classrooms with happy, cooperative children. If they are used properly, they can become teachable moments. For examples of transition activities, please visit the Early Childhood/ Family Education Web site at <http://sde.state.ok.us> and look under the "helpful forms" link.

Helpful Hints for Smooth Transitions
- Give adequate warnings before the next activity.
- Follow the daily schedule as closely as possible. Young children thrive on routine when they know what to do and what is expected. Flexibility means shortening or lengthening a part of a day, not changing the schedule entirely. Always prepare children before "special" changes occur.
- Plan carefully. Collect materials before the activity. Think through each transition and build transition activities into your daily plan.
- Link transition signals to specific activities.
- Use songs and finger plays.
- Keep a notebook or a file box of transition activities.

Group Time

Group time is one of the most important time of the day. During this time, the teacher, the teacher assistant and the children come together as a community developing trust and acceptance as they share, learn, listen, and participate in meaningful activities. Group time that follows predictable patterns consistent throughout the year allows students to gain the confidence that comes from knowing what to expect. Group time provides children with information, skills, concepts, and strategies necessary for success when working independently and in small groups.

Guidelines for Group Time
- The length of group time is determined by the age and development of the children. At the beginning of the year, group time may last only ten or fifteen minutes.
- Have clear objectives for each group activity and gather all materials needed in advance.
- Create a balance of activities that include listening, singing, discussing and moving. Provide opportunities for choral and individual responses.
- Relate the activities to children's past experiences and prior knowledge.
- Let children be the guide for determining the success of an activity. Lengthen or shorten the time as student interest indicates.

Suggested Activities for Group Time
- Morning meeting
- Calendar and weather
- Read aloud
- Picture / Vocabulary development
- Rhyming activities
- Problem-solving activities
- Phonological awareness for Pre-kindergarten or alphabet and word wall activities in Kindergarten
- Movement activities (songs, finger plays, rhythms and games)
- Group games

- Student sharing
- Class community meeting
- Introduction of new concepts
- Guest speakers
- Modeling the appropriate use and care of classroom materials
- Group writing activities
- Review of classroom rules

Notes

1. Learning experiences should be planned so teacher-initiated or child-initiated opportunities exist in small group contexts for acquiring new skills.

应该计划好学习经历，以便在获得新技能的小群体环境中，能够存在教师发起或儿童发起的机会。

2. Alternate active and less active learning moments rather than lengthy periods of sitting still.

交替安排活跃的和活动量小的学习时段，而不是长时间久坐不动。

less active：低活动的，不活跃的。形容词 active 的比较级，

e.g. We are focusing on less active work. 我们集中注意在不活跃的工作上。

3. Respect the need for young children to rest or be active as is appropriate and does not compromise quality learning time. 尊重幼儿适当休息或者适当活动的需要，不能让学习时间的质量打折扣。

as is appropriate 适用

e.g. It is bigger and more comprehensive, as is appropriate for a country preparing for the disasters we have described. 这次更大更全面，适用于一个国家准备应对我们描述的灾难。

4. Reflect integrated teaching rather than class time separated subject by subject.

体现整合教学，而不是以学科来划分课堂时间。

5. Allow for smooth transitions between activities or classrooms, with the teacher capitalizing on these transitions as learning moments.

要安排好活动之间或课堂之间的顺利转换，教师应将这些转换当成学习的时间。

allow for 把……考虑进去，顾及，为……留有余地；估计到

e.g. to allow for the difference in their ages 考虑到他们年龄的差异

6. Group time that follows predictable patterns consistent throughout the year allows students to gain the confidence that comes from knowing what to expect.

集体时间的模式应该保持一年不变，这样儿童会因为预先了解后面要进行的活动而产生自信。

此句是一个复杂的复合句：主语（Group time）+ 定语从句（that... the year）+ 谓语（allows）+ 宾语（students）+ 宾补（to... confidence）+ 定语从句（that... to expect）

7. Relate the activities to children's past experiences and prior knowledge.

将活动与儿童过去的经历和先前的知识联系起来。

relate... to 涉及；同……有……关系；与……协调；将……与……联系起来

e.g. And I know how to relate that to a constant. 我知道如何把它和一个常数联系起来。

8. Phonological awareness for Pre-kindergarten or alphabet and word wall activities in Kindergarten.

日托生的音韵意识或幼儿园字母和单词墙活动

Pre-Kindergarten: day care with some educational content for children younger than five, provided by elementary schools or pre-schools. 由小学或幼儿园提供的，配有适合5岁以下儿童教育内容的日托所。

e.g. Both beginning and experienced teachers, from pre-kindergarten through elementary, will find a wealth of appropriate materials and suggestions.
从日托所到小学，初学者和经验丰富的老师都会找到丰富的材料和建议。

Useful Words & Expressions

curriculum [kəˈrɪkjʊləm] *n.* 课程，总课程
open-ended [ˌəʊpənˈendɪd] *adj.* 开放式的
schedule [ˈʃedjuːl] *vt.* 安排，计划；编制目录
　　　　　　　　　n. 时间表；计划表；一览表
teacher-directed [ˈtiːtʃə dɪˈrektɪd] *adj.* 以教师为主导的
consistency [kənˈsɪst(ə)nsi] *n.* 一致性；连贯性
flexible [ˈfleksəbl] *adj.* 灵活的；柔韧的；易弯的
portion [ˈpɔːʃ(ə)n] *n.* 部分；一份；命运
　　　　　　　　　vt. 分配；给……嫁妆
prioritize [praɪˈɒrətaɪz] *vt.* 优先处理；按重要性排列
self-expression [ˌself-ɪksˈpreʃn] *n.* 自我表现
alternate [ˈɔːltəneɪt] *vt.* 使交替；使轮流 *n.* 替换物
　　　　　[ɔːlˈtɜːnət] *adj.* 交替的；轮流的
lengthy [ˈleŋθɪ] *adj.* 冗长的；啰唆的
integrate [ˈɪntɪɡreɪt] *vt.* 使一体化；使整合，使完整
　　　　　　　　　adj. 整体的；完整的；综合的
ample [ˈæmpl] *adj.* 充足的，丰富的；富裕的
transition [trænˈzɪʃn] *n.* 过渡，转变，变迁
capitalize on 充分利用某事物；从某事物中获利
take pride in 为……感到自豪，以……骄傲
accomplishment [əˈkʌmplɪʃmənt] *n.* 成就；完成
collaborative [kəˈlæbərətɪv] *adj.* 协作的；合作的
prompt [prɒmpt] *v.* 提示；促使；导致；鼓励

"attention getters" 吸引注意妙法
signal [ˈsɪɡnəl] *n.* 信号；预兆；导火线
　　　　　　　　vt. 向……发信号；以信号告知
teachable moment 可用于教学的时间
hint [hɪnt] *n.* 暗示，线索，迹象，提示，注意事项
adequate [ˈædɪkwət] *adj.* 充足的；适当的；胜任的
thrive on 乐于做某事，靠吃……长壮；喜欢……
routine [ruːˈtiːn] *n.* 常规；日常；例行程序
　　　　　　　　adj. 常规的；例行的；日常的；普通的
flexibility [ˌfleksəˈbɪləti] *n.* 灵活性；可塑度
build ... into 使成为……的一部分
acceptance [əkˈseptəns] *n.* 接受，接纳；赞成
predictable [prɪˈdɪktəbl] *adj.* 可预见的；可预言的
consistent [kənˈsɪstənt] *adj.* 一致的；连续的
strategy [ˈstrætədʒi] *n.* 策略，战略；战略学
guideline [ˈɡaɪdlaɪn] *n.* 指导原则；指南
choral and individual responses 齐声与个别回答
rhyming activity 韵律活动
phonological [ˌfɒnəˈlɒdʒɪkl] *adj.* 音韵学的
awareness [əˈweənəs] *n.* 察觉，觉悟，意识
alphabet [ˈælfəbet] *n.* 字母表；字母系统；入门
pre-kindergarten [priːˌkɪndəˈɡaːtən] *adj.* 进幼儿园前的，幼小的

Ideological and Political Concept

学习环境是一种重要而强大的教学工具。幼教工作者应在了解幼儿学习和发展规律的基础上创建科学的学习环境，那么这样的环境就能对教学起到促进作用。在创建科学适当的学习环境方面，不能忽略育人格局，应在幼儿自主探索和集中教育活动的设计中融入国家民族认同感教育，例如国家的地理位置、象征、标志性建筑、人物形象、文化传统和道德价值观的渗透。

Part 3 English Proficiency

Word Building (Ⅳ) 构词（四）

Derivation Ⅲ——派生法（三）
Suffix—后缀

> 加后缀通常会改变单词的词类，构成意义相近的其他词性的词，少数后缀还会改变词义，变为与原来词义相反的新词。

Adjectives & Adverbs 形容词和副词

Part of Speech		Suffix	Meaning	Examples
Adjective 形容词	n. → adj.	-ed	having 有……的	simple-mind**ed** 头脑简单的；blue-ey**ed** 蓝眼睛的；odd-shap**ed** 奇形怪状的
		-ful	full of; providing 富有……的；供给……的	use**ful** 有用的；meaning**ful** 有意义的；success**ful** 成功的；help**ful** 有帮助的
		-ish	somewhat like 近于……的	child**ish** 幼稚的；fool**ish** 愚蠢的；snobb**ish** 势利眼的；Engl**ish** 英语的
		-less	without 无	care**less** 粗心的；meaning**less** 无意义的；harm**less** 无害的；home**less** 无家的
		-like	like……般	child**like** 孩子般的；monkey**like**（猴子般的）；statesman**like** 政治家般的
		-ly	having the qualities of 具有……品质的	friend**ly** 友好的；mother**ly** 慈母般的；coward**ly** 胆小的；dai**ly** 每天的
	v. → adj.	-able	of the kind that is subject to being v.-ed 受动的	accept**able** 能接受的；wash**able** 能洗的；drink**able** 能喝的；manage**able** 可管理的
		-ive		attract**ive** 吸引人的；effect**ive** 有效的；possess**ive** 拥有的；product**ive** 多产的
Adverb 副词	adj. → adv.	-ly	in a... manner/respect; to a degree ……状态；……程度	personal**ly** 亲自地；calm**ly** 平静地；kind**ly** 好心地；eager**ly** 急切地；simp**ly** 简单地
	n. → adv.	-wise	in... way 可用于表示方式、尺度 as far as... is concerned / so far as... is concerned 在……方面（作状语）	clock**wise** 顺时针方向地；crab**wise** 横斜地；cross**wise** 十字形地 weather**wise** 就天气而言；education**wise** 就教育而言；tax**wise** 就税收而言 Dollar**wise**, business is better than ever, but not so good profit**wise**. 从成交的美元数额来看，生意确实比过去兴隆了，但是从利润方面来看，情况不见得比过去好。

Adjective 形容词

表示人或事物的属性、特征或状态的词叫形容词。形容词修饰名词或代词，一般放在所修饰的词之前。

1. 形容词的句法作用

作用	示例
作定语	It's a **sunny** day today. 今天天气晴朗。 Mary is a **nice** girl. 玛丽是个可爱的女孩。
作表语	He looks **happy** today. 他今天看上去很高兴。 I feel **tired** after playing football. 踢球之后我觉得累。 He turned **red** when he heard the news. 当他听到这个消息时，他脸红了。 It's going to stay **cold** for some time. 它会在一段时间内保持低温。 The beer tastes very **delicious**. 这啤酒味道很好。 He was **asleep**. 他睡着了。 become come fall get go grow make turn （变成某种状态） continue hold keep lie remain stay （保持某种状态） appear feel look smell sound taste know （感觉）
表语形容词 （只作表语）	(✓) Don't be **afraid**.　　　　　　　　(✗) Mr Li is an afraid man. (✓) The old man was **ill** yesterday.　 (✗) This is an ill person. (✓) This place is **worth** visiting.　　　(✗) That is a worth book.
定语形容词 （只作定语）	(✓) My **elder** brother is a doctor.　　(✗) My brother is elder than I. (✓) This is a **little** house.　　　　　　(✗) The house is little. (✓) Do you want **live** fish or dead one.　(✗) The old monkey is still live.
补足语	The door was left **unlocked**. 门没锁。（主补） Don't keep the door **open**. 不要让门开着。（宾补） His success made him **happy**. 他的成功让他很开心。（宾补）
受副词修饰	The girl is **extremely** pretty. 这个女孩非常漂亮。 He had an **unusually** deep voice. 他的声音异常低沉。
the+ 形容词 （见定冠词）	**The old** often think of old things. 老人们常常想起往事。 **The new** always take the place of the old. 新的（事物）总会取代旧的。
作状语 （代替副词）	He came home, **dead** tired. 他回到家来，累得要死。 Their child finally got home **sate and sound**. 他们的小孩终于安然无恙地回到家。
比较级 最高级	Your room is twice **as large as** mine. 你的房间是我的两倍大。 He is not **as/so tall as** me. 他没我高。 Jackie is **taller** than Alex, but Alex is **heavier** than Jackie. 杰基比亚历克斯高，但亚历克斯比杰基重。 He is getting **more and more handsome**. 他越来越帅。 I feel much **better** now. 我现在感觉好多了。 He is **the strongest** in our class. 他是我们班里身体最强壮的。 It was **the most/least interesting** story I have ever listened to. 这是我听过的最有趣/最无趣的故事。

2. 形容词作定语的位置

位置	特征	示例
后置	以 -ible /-able 结尾	It's the only solution **possible**. 这是唯一可能采取的解决办法。 Are there any tickets **available**? 还有票吗? That's the only star **visible** now. 那是颗现在唯一可见的星。
	形容词短语	I know an actor **suitable for the part**. (*adj.*+ *prep*. phrase) 我认识一个适合扮演这个角色的演员。 It is a problem **difficult to work out**. 这是一个难以解决的问题。(*adj*. + to do)
	修饰不定代词	They are discussing something **important**. 他们正在讨论重要的事情。 Anyone **intelligent** can do it. 任何有头脑的人都能做这件事。 I know it's nothing **serious**. 我知道那根本没什么大不了的。 Do you know anybody **else** here? 这儿你还认识别的人吗? He found his son with everything **necessary**. 他供给他儿子一切必需品。
	成对使用	Visitors, **old and young**, were delighted. 不管老少, 所有的参观者都很高兴。 There was a huge cupboard, **simple and beautiful**. 有一个大食橱, 简朴而美观。
可前可后	意义不变	a **possible** way. 一种可能的方法 in every way **possible** 一切可能的方式 every **available** doctor 所有能找到的医生 the options **available** 可用的选项
	意义不同	the writer **present** 出席的作家 the **present** writer 当代的作家 an **involved** father 一个投入的父亲 the people **involved** 参与的人 He is a **responsible** man. 他是一个负责任的人。 The man **responsible** should be their manager. 负责任的应该是他们的经理。

3. 多个形容词作定语的位置排序

限定词（冠词→指示代词→形容词性物主代词→名词所有格）
↓
数词
↓
描绘性形容词（大小→长短→高低→年龄→新旧→颜色）
↓
出处（国籍→地区）
↓
特质（物质→材料→用途）
↓
名词（中心词）

e.g. **an exciting international football** match 一场令人激动的国际足球赛

a new red sports shirt 一件新的红色运动衫

a light black plastic umbrella 一把轻的黑塑料伞

a small old brown wooden house 一座又小又旧的棕色木头房子

two big round new Chinese wooden tables 两张新的中国式木制大圆桌

his large new black foreign car 他那辆新的大型黑色外国轿车

Adverb 副词

副词是一种用来修饰动词、形容词或全句的词，是说明时间、地点、程度、方式等概念的词。

1. 除副词本身外，形容词转变为副词的构成方式

词尾	变化	示例
	+ly	careful → carefully polite → politely wide → widely
-le	-le → -ly	terrible → terribly gentle → gently simple → simply possible → possibly
-y [i]	-y → i+ly	happy → happily heavy → heavily angry → angrily busy → busily
-ic	-ic → ic+ally	economic-economically basic-basically scientific-scientifically automatic-automatically energetic-energetically
-ly = adj. (≠ adv.)		friendly deadly lovely lonely likely lively ugly brotherly
adj.=adv.		better last early more else much far next fast only hard well straight high deep wide firm close daily weekly monthly yearly
Exceptions（特例）		public → publicly full → fully whole → wholly true → truly sole → solely

2. 副词的种类及作用

种类	作用
Manner 方式	Jack drives very *carefully*. 杰克开车非常小心。（修饰动词） He won the tennis match *effortlessly*. 他毫不费力就赢了网球比赛。（修饰动词） *She slowly* opened the present. 她慢慢打开了礼物。（修饰动词） I must be *off* now. 我现在得走了。（表语）
Time 时间	We'll let you know our decision *next week*. 下周我们会通知你我们的决定。 I flew to Dallas three weeks *ago*. 三个星期前我飞去了达拉斯。（修饰全句）
Frequency 频率	My father *usually* walks home. 我的父亲经常步行回家。（修饰全句） I will *always* love you. 我将永远爱你。（修饰全句） *Sometimes* I go to school by bus. 我有时坐公交车上学。（修饰全句） I go to school by bike *usually*. 我通常骑车上学。（修饰全句） Do you *often* go there? 你常去那里吗？（修饰全句） *Never* have I been there. 我从未去过那里。（倒装句，修饰全句）
Degree 程度	They like playing golf *a lot*. 他们很喜欢打高尔夫。（修饰动词） She doesn't enjoy watching TV *at all*. 她一点都不喜欢看电视。（修饰动词） She *nearly* flew to Boston. 她差点就飞去波士顿了。（修饰动词） I don't know him *well enough*. 我不太了解他。（*enough* 修饰副词 well）
Place 地点	I'm going *nowhere*. 我停滞不前。（地点状语） She found the box *outside*. 她在外面发现了这个箱子。（宾补） The people *here* are very friendly. 这里的人们都很友好。（修饰名词，后置定语） They live a village *nearby*. 他们住在附近的村子里。（修饰名词，后置定语） There is a TV set in the room *upstairs*. 楼上的房间有一台电视机。（后置定语） Is your mother *in*? 你妈妈在家吗？（表语）

3. 副词的比较级和最高级

等级	例句
比较级	Tom runs *as quickly as* Bob. 汤姆跑得和鲍伯一样快。 I don't write *as/so well as* Alice. 我不像爱丽丝写得那么好。 She can read *twice as fast as* he does. 她阅读的速度比他快一倍。 He'll come back *sooner or later*. 他迟早会回来的。 Please speak *more slowly*. 请讲慢一点。 I had seen the film only a few days *earlier*. 我是几天前才看的这部电影。 He works *less than* he used to. 他工作的时间比以前少了。 Can you come over *a bit more quickly*? 你能稍微快点来吗?
最高级	He laughs *best* who laughs *last*.（谚语）谁笑到最后谁笑得最好。 Of the four of us, I sang *(the) worst*. 我们四人中，我唱得最差。 Tom runs *the most quickly* in that group. 汤姆在那群人中跑得最快。

Part 4　Unit Practice

1. Read aloud and write down the following words according to the phonics.

autumn /awful /break / sheep / theatre / receive / height /again /pleasure / journey

[pleɪ] _____　　　　　[greɪt] _____　　　　　[bred] _____

[θriː] _____　　　　　[ˈmʌŋki] _____　　　　　[njuː] _____

2. Put the school languages into English.

大家坐成圆圈。　　　　　　　　　　圆圈时间不要玩耍。请遵守规则！

请注意！　　　　　　　　　　　　　我喜欢杰瑞的坐姿。

我们来做沉默游戏。　　　　　　　　请回到你的座位。

3. Put the following phrases and sentences into Chinese.

（1）to evaluate the daily schedule, classroom arrangement, materials within each learning center, and the curriculum.

（2）creating a positive early childhood environment

（3）The classroom should be organized to foster exploration with learning materials.

（4）Learning materials should be concrete and relevant to a child's own life experiences (open-ended but purposeful).

（5）The classroom environment should be set up for choices.

4. Read the derived words and name them.

simple-mind**ed** _____　　　　wire**less** _____　　　　calm**ly** _____

use**ful** _____　　　　　　　　monkey**like** _____　　　clock**wise** _____

child**ish** _____　　　　　　　drink**able** _____　　　　friend**ly** _____

5. Chose the best answer to complete the sentences.

(1) Tony is going camping with _____ boys.
   A. little two other　　　　　　　　B. two little other
   C. two other little　　　　　　　　D. little other two

(2) One day they crossed the _____ bridge behind the palace.
   A. old Chinese stone　　　　　　　B. Chinese old stone
   C. old stone Chinese　　　　　　　D. Chinese stone old

(3) —How was your recent visit to Qingdao?
   —It was great. We visited some friends, and spent the _____ days at the seaside.
   A. few last sunny　　B. last few sunny　　C. last sunny few　　D. few sunny last

(4) —Are you feeling _____?
   —Yes, I'm fine now.
   A. any well　　　　B. any better　　　　C. quite good　　　　D. quite better

(5) The experiment was _____ easier than we had expected.
   A. more　　　　　　B. much more　　　　C. much　　　　　　　D. more much

(6) If there were no examinations, we should have _____ at school.
   A. the happiest time　　　　　　　B. a more happier time
   C. much happiest time　　　　　　D. a much happier time

(7) The weather in China is different from _____.
   A. in America　　　B. one in America　　C. America　　　　　D. that in America

(8) After the new technique was introduced, the factory produced _____ tractors in 1988 as the year before.
   A. as twice many　　B. as many twice　　C. twice as many　　D. twice many as

(9) John has three sisters, Mary is the _____ of the three.
   A. most cleverest　　B. more clever　　　C. cleverest　　　　D. cleverer

(10) She told us _____ story that we all forget about the time.
   A. such an interesting　　　　　　B. such interesting a
   C. so an interesting　　　　　　　D. a so interesting

Part 5　Extended Reading

Technology Center

　　The Technology Center is a valuable addition to the early childhood classroom if it is set up with knowledge of children's development as well as knowledge of the equipment and available software. Your Technology Center will only be as good as the materials in it, so consider this item carefully before purchasing the equipment. Adult interaction is the key to a successful Technology Center.

Child Development

The Technology Center offers many experiences to facilitate growth and enhance skills in all areas of development.

Physical Skills: enhance fine motor development by using the keyboard and manipulating the mouse, eye-hand coordination and visual perception to track on the screen and move the cursor.

Social/Emotional Skills: promote responsibility, cooperation, working with others and persistence.

Language Skills: increase vocabulary and knowledge of print by linking words to pictures.

Intellectual Skills: develop cause-and-effect by observing what happens on the keyboard, following directions, and a variety of other skills depending on the software selected.

Points to Remember

- Introduce the computer or other technology to one or two children at a time.
- Observe the children, so you know how to discuss and interact with them to further their level of use.
- Ask open-ended questions which focus on what they are doing.
- Consult *Survey of Early Childhood Software* by Warren Buckleitner, published by the High Scope Educations Research Foundation, for appropriate software.
- Consult *Creative Curriculum* by Dodge and Colker for comprehensive information about setting up a technology center.

Suggested Technology Center Materials

Computer screen	Compact disks
Mouse	Compact disk player
Hard drive	Digital video disks
Surge protector	Digital video player
Computer table	Magnifying glasses
Sufficient power and electrical outlets	Binoculars
Mouse pad	Telephone
Appropriate software programs	MP3 player
Table	Radio
Camera	Speaker
Video cameras	Label maker
Tape recorders	Light show props
Word processing programs	Calculators
Class website	Weather station
Web design programs	Thermometer
Educational video games	Analog clock
Television	Digital clock
Video player	Watches

Learning Environment II

> "What we want is to see the child in pursuit of knowledge, and not knowledge in pursuit of the child."
> —George Bernard Shaw

Learning Objectives

Students will
- ★ review vowel digraph sounds
- ★ be familiar with school languages, chants, songs and stories
- ★ learn how to play a game for children
- ★ master new words and expressions
- ★ learn how to set up the learning environment for children's independence and a joy of learning
- ★ review compounding words and prepositions

UNIT 5

Part 1 Skills for Pre-school English Teaching

English Phonics Ⅳ 自然拼读法（四）

Vowel Digraph Sounds (Part 2) 元音字母组合的读音 (2)

Vowel Digraph		Sounds & Examples		
		Long Vowel		Short Vowel
Ii	ia	[aɪə] [ɪə]	dialogue giant trial via Australia India material	
	ie	[iː] [aɪə] [ɪə]	believe field piece thief quiet science variety experience nutrient	[ɪ] auntie cookie sweetie
	io	[aɪə] [ɪəu] [jə] [ɪə]	lion pioneer riot violin audio Mario radio studio companion million opinion idiot idiom period	[ə] religion suspicion fashion
	iu	[ɪə]	stadium genius radium	

Language Activities 语言活动

- Today, I'm going to share a story with you.
  今天我要给你们讲一个故事。
- What's the name of the story/chant?
  这个故事（儿歌）的名字是什么？
- What happens in the story?
  故事里面发生了什么事？
- I'll show you some pictures.
  我要给你们看一些图片。
- Raise / Put up your hands if you have any questions.
  有问题请举手。
- Who wants to try? / Who wants to have a try?
  谁来试一下？

81

- Read after me. / Say it after me.
  跟我读。
- Let's act out the story.
  我们来把故事演出来。
- Can you speak a little louder?
  你可以大点声说吗?
- Can you say it again?
  你可以再说一遍吗?
- May I ask for a volunteer?
  有没有人主动发言?
- Whose turn? / Who is the next?
  轮到谁了? /下一个是谁?
- Shall we begin / start now?
  现在可以开始吗?
- Do you like it? / Is it funny?
  你们喜欢这个故事吗? /有趣吗?

 Chants & Songs

Days of the Week & Months of the Year 星期月份

Sunday, Monday

Tuesday, Wednesday

Thursday, Friday

Saturday

January, February, March and April

May and June and July and August

September, October, November, December

These are the months of the year.

Chants & Songs

Ten Little Indians

1. One little two little three little Indi-ans, four little five little six little Indi-ans,
2. One thin two thin three thin tea-chers, four thin five thin six thin tea-chers,
3. One tall two tall three tall doc-tors, four tall five tall six tall doc-tors,
4. One fat two fat three fat nur-ses, four fat five fat six fat nur-ses,
5. One short two short three short pi-lots, four short five short six short pi-lots,

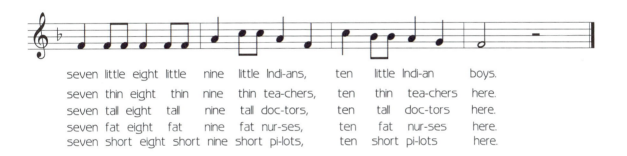

seven little eight little nine little Indi-ans, ten little Indi-an boys.
seven thin eight thin nine thin tea-chers, ten thin tea-chers here.
seven tall eight tall nine tall doc-tors, ten tall doc-tors here.
seven fat eight fat nine fat nur-ses, ten fat nur-ses here.
seven short eight short nine short pi-lots, ten short pi-lots here.

OPEN THEM, SHUT THEM

Open them, shut them, open them, shut them,

Give a little clap,

Open them, shut them, open them, shut them,

Put them in your lap.

Creep them, creep them, creep them, creep them,

Right up to your chin,

Open up your little mouth,

But do not put them in.

Open them, shut them, open them, shut them,

Give a little clap,

Open them, shut them, open them, shut them,

Put them in your lap.

Creep them, creep them, creep them, creep them,

Right up to your cheek,

Cover up your little eyes,

And through your fingers peek.

- Infant—Do hand motions as poem indicates.
- Toddler—Have child mimic your actions.

I Will Not Take a Bath 我不想洗澡

I will not take a bath, I won't get in the tub, I had a bath last week. I don't need another scrub.

I would need my rubber duck, bucket and a boat, my toy whale, a submarine, a rubber ball.

Now, I cannot take a bath. The tub is too small. It's all filled up with toys. There's no room for me.

I Want to Be Your Mommy 我想成为你的妈妈

One day, a mother asked her children what their dreams are. "What do you want to be when you grow up?" she asked them. The first child answered, "I want to be Superman. I want to be the strongest person in the world." The second child answered, "I want to be a doctor. I want to help sick people."

The mother asked her youngest child, "What do you want to be?" The child answered, "I want to be your mommy. I want to hug you when you get home from school. I want to cook rice for you when

you're hungry. I want to sit by your pillow all night looking after you when you're sick, just like you do for me."

Whisper 悄悄话

Objective: Listening

Steps: 1. Get two teams of children.

2. The teacher whispers a word / sentence to the first child of each team.

3. The child quickly turns to the next and whispers whatever he / she heard from the teacher. Others from both teams will do the same.

4. The last child from each team will shout it out so that the teacher checks the correctness.

5. The faster and correct team wins.

Tips: 1. Make sure that all the children must pass the word / sentence in low voice.

2. Better not to put too many children in a team.

Language: Let's play whisper game. I'll tell you a very important message, and you must pass it one by one to your friends as fast as you can, but only by whispering. The last child should shout it out. Is that clear for everybody?

Part 2 Pre-school Education in English

Setting Up the Learning Environment

The environment of the classroom communicates to students what is expected of them. Independence and a joy of learning are what should be conveyed. In the early childhood classroom, the use of learning centers is a key component to ensure the success of students.

Classroom Arrangement

When planning where to set up centers, take a close look at your classroom. Three basic settings are needed: a place for the whole class to work together, a place for students to work independently, and a place for teacher-directed small group work. It is helpful to use a map of the classroom with scale cutouts of furniture and equipment to try different arrangements. Once you have set up your room and observed students in the environment, it may be necessary to do some rearranging to better accommodate their needs.

Keep the following considerations in mind:

- Create logical traffic patterns so students can move about easily from one area of the room to another without disturbing others.
- Consider fixed items such as sinks, built-in shelves, carpeted and tiled flooring, and electrical outlets; use space efficiently.
- Separate quiet and noisy activities.
- Provide a large floor space for group activities.
- Create an area for teacher-directed small group activities.
- Provide space for individual work.
- Store appropriate materials and equipment near the center in which they will be used.

Suggested Learning Centers

The following is a list of centers that are typically found in the early childhood classroom. Suggested materials and activities are included in the discussion of the center areas.

Art Center	Block Center
Literacy Center	Dramatic Play Center
Library Center	Music and Movement Center
Listening Center	Cooking Center
Writing Center	Computer Center
Math Center	Woodworking Center
Science and Sensory Center	

Pre-kindergarten classrooms may want to combine Language, Literacy, Math, and Science centers into one large Game Center.

Guidelines for Learning Centers

Materials in learning centers are selected and arranged to foster involvement, independence, decision making, and responsibility. Students are given extended opportunities to practice these skills by selecting and using the materials offered at each center. To ensure the success of students and centers in the classroom, the following guidelines are suggested:

- Introduce each learning center with discussions regarding rules, use of materials, and responsibilities.
- Students can be scheduled into centers using a rotation system or a self-selected system. When using a rotation system, students move through centers in small groups in a systematic way. When using a self-selected system, students move themselves through the centers.
- All learning centers have a broad range of activities to accommodate each student's interest and level of development.
- The skill level in each center increases during the year through a variety of open-ended activities.
- Always model new activities.
- Define center boundaries with low shelves, carpet, or tape.
- Organize materials on low shelves close to their point of use so the materials in each center are always accessible to the students.
- Organize small items in labeled tubs or baskets for easy clean-up.
- Utilize a sign to describe the skills learned while working in each center.
- Place pictures, words, or outlines of objects on shelves to assist students in putting materials away when an activity is completed.

Classroom

The outdoor environment can also be an extension of the indoor classroom where learning blossoms. For this to be possible, add the following equipment to your classroom.

- Sand and water table
- Fence or free-standing easels (paint the flower you can see)
- Book tub on wheels (read in the shade of a tree)
- Dramatic play materials:
    — Barbecue Center
    — Picnic Table and Basket
    — Tent
    — Gardening Center
- Science discovery tools (magnifying glasses, binoculars, butterfly nets, bug catching equipment)
- Woodworking materials
- Almost anything on wheels

Notes

1. The environment of the classroom communicates to students what is expected of them.

教室的环境向学生传达对他们的期望。

is expected of 对……的期待，预期

e.g. Better understand assignments and what is expected of you.

更好地理解任务，以及别人对你的期待。

2. ... it may be necessary to do some rearranging to better accommodate their needs.

为了更好地适应他们的需要，可能有必要进行一些重新安排。

Syntactical analysis：形式主语（it）＋谓语（系表）（may be necessary）＋真主语（to do... needs）；

真主语结构中 to better accommodate their needs 作目的状语，better 是副词 well 的比较级。

3. Materials in learning centers are selected and arranged to foster involvement, independence, decision making, and responsibility. 学习中心材料的选择和布置是为了促进参与、独立、决策和责任。

4. Organize materials on low shelves close to their point of use so the materials in each center are always accessible to the students.

将材料摆放在较低的架子上，靠近他们的使用点，这样学生们总是可以随时无障碍使用每个中心的材料。

5. The outdoor environment can also be an extension of the indoor classroom where learning blossoms.

室外环境也可以是学习活动集中的室内教室的延伸。

6. sand and water table 沙水台

儿童户外玩沙子和水的桌子。如下图。

Useful Words & Expressions

convey [kənˈveɪ] *vt.* 表达；传达，传递；运送

component [kəmˈpəʊnənt] *n.* 成分；零件；[数] 要素

take a close look at 仔细看看，深入了解

setting [ˈsetɪŋ] *n.* 环境；镶嵌；装置；（某事、戏剧、小说等的）背景

scale [skeɪl] *n*. 规模；比例；刻度；天平
cutout [ˈkʌtˌaʊt] *n*. 剪下的图样；剪纸
scale cutout 按比例剪下的图样
accommodate [əˈkɒmədeɪt] *vt*. 容纳；使适应；供应
　　　　　　　　　　　　　vi. 适应；调解
logical traffic pattern 合理的交通模式
fix [fɪks] *vt*. 使固定；修理；安装；准备
item [ˈaɪtəm] *n*. 项目；条目；条款；一件商品
fixed item 固定的物品
built-in [bɪltˈɪn] *adj*. 内置的；固有的；嵌入的
carpet [ˈkɑːpɪt] *n*. 地毯，桌毯；毛毯，绒毯；地毯
　　　　　　　　vt. 在……上铺地毯
tile [taɪl] *n*. 瓦片；瓷砖；空心砖；麻将牌
　　　　　　vt. 用瓦片、瓷砖等覆盖
carpeted and tiled flooring 铺地毯和瓷砖的地面
electrical outlet 插座
typically [ˈtɪpɪkli] *adv*. 通常；典型地；代表性地

sensory [ˈsensəri] *adj*. 感觉的，感受的，感官的
Science and Sensory Center 科学与感知中心
foster involvement 促进参与
define [dɪˈfaɪn] *vt*. 规定；使明确
boundary [ˈbaʊndri] *n*. 分界线；范围；边线
accessible [əkˈsesəbl] *adj*. 易接近的；可理解的
utilize [ˈjuːtɪˌlaɪz] *vt*. 利用
outline [ˈaʊtlaɪn] *n*. 轮廓；大纲；概要；略图
　　　　　　　　　vt. 概述；略述；描画……轮廓
opportune [ˈɒpətjuːn] *adj*. 适时的；（时间）合适的
　　　　　　　　　　　adv. 恰好地，适时地
　　　　　　　　　　　n. 恰好，适时，及时
blossom [ˈblɒsəm] *vi*. 开花；兴旺；发展成长
easel [ˈiːzl] *n*. 画架，黑板架
free-standing easel 独立的画架
magnify [ˈmæɡnɪfaɪ] *vt*.& *vi*. 放大；赞美；夸大

Ideological and Political Concept

　　在学前教育的课堂中，学习中心（区角活动）的使用是保证幼儿探索学习成功的关键因素。在幼儿园五大学科领域相关的区域或角落活动的设计中应融入科学精神和人文精神教育，培养求真求实、批判创新的精神和平等尊重、互助合作、遵守规则的意识。启发幼儿深入探索自然现象、深刻理解社会现象。

Part 3　English Proficiency

Morphology

Word Building Ⅴ 构词（五）

Compounding—合成法

> Compounding is a process of word formation by which two or more stems are put together to make one word. The word formed in this way is called a compound.
> 合成法是将两个或更多的词干放在一起形成一个单词，这样形成的词称为合成词。

1. Nouns 合成为名词

n.+*n.*	website 网站；weekend 周末
n.+*v.*	daybreak 黎明；snowfall 下雪
n.+*ger.*	horse-riding 骑马；handwriting 书法
n.+*prep.*+*n.*	daughter-in-law 儿媳
ger.+*n.*	waiting-room 候车
ppr.+*n.*	flying-fish 飞鱼；falling-leaf 落叶
adj.+*n.*	greenhouse 温室；freshman 大一新生
adv.+*n.*	income 收入；outlook 景色，风光
prep.+*n.*	afternoon 下午；afterbrain 后脑
pp.+*adv.*	grown-up 成年人
n.+*vt.*+er/or	pain-killer 止痛药
v.+*n.*	typewriter 打字机
pron.+*n.*	she-wolf 母狼

2. Adjectives 合成为形容词

n.+*adj.* world-famous 世界闻名的；blood-red 血红的
n.+*ppr.* peace-loving 热爱和平的
n.+*pp.* heart-broken 伤心的；man-made 人造的
v.+*adv.* takeaway 外卖的
adj.+*n.* long-distance 长途的；high-quality 高质量的
adj.+*n.* + *pp.* noble-minded 高尚的
adj.+*adj.* dark-blue 深蓝色的
adj.+*ppr.* ordinary-looking 相貌一般的
adj.+*pp.* new-born 新出生的
adv.+*adj.* ever-green 常青的

adv.+*ppr.* hard-working 勤劳的
adv.+*pp.* well-known 著名的
adv.+*n.* downstairs 楼下的
num.+*n.* first-class 头等的；one-way 单行道的
num.+*n.*+*adj.* ten-year-old 十岁大的
num.+*n.*+*pp.* three-cornered 三角的
prep.+*n.* indoor 室内的
n.+to+*n.* one-to-one 一对一的
num.+*adv.* one-off 一次性的

3. Adverbs 合成为副词

adj.+ *n.* hotfoot 匆忙地
adj.+*adv.* everywhere 到处
adv.+*adv.* however 尽管如此

prep.+*n.* beforehand 事先
prep. +*adv.* forever 永远
adv.+*n.* upstairs 在楼上

4. Verbs 合成为动词

n.+*v.* water-cool 用水冷却；sleep-walk 梦游
adj.+*v.* quick-charge 快速充电；white-wash 粉刷
adv.+*v.* outact 行动上胜过；download 下载

Preposition 介词

介词是一种用来表示词与词，或者词与句之间关系的词，在句中不能单独作成分。介词一定要有宾语，充当宾语的一般有名词、代词或相当于名词的其他词、短语或从句。

1. 介词的种类

   （1）简单介词，如 at, in, off, on, by, to, with 等。

   （2）合成介词，如 into, inside, within, throughout 等。

   （3）短语介词，如 according to, because of, in addition to, in front of, in spite of 等。

2. 介词的宾语类型

名词	Let's go for *a walk* along *the river*. 咱们到江边散散步。
代词	He's standing in front of *me*. 他站在我前面。
形容词	Her pronunciation is far from (being) *perfect*. 她的语音远不完美。 Recently, I had a wonderful experience that outsiders may regard as (being) *incredible*. 我最近经历了一件很奇妙的事，外人听了可能会觉得不可思议。
动名词	He's good at *drawing*. 他擅长绘画。 Thank you for *coming*. 谢谢你来。
过去分词	I took it for *granted* that she was from England. 我还以为她是来自英国的。 After a few rounds of talks, both sides regarded the territory dispute as *settled*. 经过几轮谈判，双方都认为领土争端已经解决。 注：过去分词只用于 take ... for granted 和 regard ... as 结构。
不定式	We had no choice except *to wait* there. 除了在那儿等，我们没有别的选择。 He *does* everything *except* washing clothes. 他除了洗衣服外，啥活都干。 We had no option but *to abandon* the meeting. 我们别无选择，只有放弃这次会面。 It *did* nothing *but* make us ridiculous. 这只是让我们显得很滑稽。 注：介词 but / except 前面有 do / does / did 时，宾语省略 to；否则不能省略 to。
疑问词＋不定式	The Prime Minister pondered on *when to go* to the polls. 首相斟酌着何时前往投票地点。
副词	I didn't know it until *recently*. 直到最近我才知道此事。
数词	He was among *the first* to arrive. 他是第一批到的。
介词短语	She won't go home until *after the exam*. 她要考完试之后再回家。
宾语从句连接代词连接副词	Think of *what I said*. 想想我说的话。 This link depends on *whether* (≠ if) the user is logged in. 此链接取决于用户是否登录。 These two pens are alike *except that* they're of different colours. 这两支笔样儿差不多，除了颜色不一样。 I'm only just beginning to take it *in that* he's still missing. 我刚刚才开始反应过来，原来他仍然下落不明。

3. 介词短语的用法

作用	示例
定语（后置）	The girl *in red* is my sister. 穿红衣的那个女孩是我妹妹。 This is her first trip *to Europe*. 这是她第一次来欧洲。 The girl *with big eyes* is Jim's sister. 大眼睛的女孩是吉姆的妹妹。
状语	She got here *at four*. 她是在4点到这儿的。（时间） We live *in Hangzhou*. 我们住在杭州。（地点） Can you say it *in English*? 这个你会用英语说吗？（方式） He ran *for shelter*. 他跑去避雨。（目的） The game was postponed *because of rain*. 因为下雨，运动会被推迟了。（原因） There will be no living things *without water*. 没有水就没有生物。（条件） They play football *in spite of the rain*. 他们冒雨踢足球。（让步） *To what extent* would you trust them? 你对他们信任程度如何？（程度）
表语	He's *in the office*. 他在办公室。 I was *at a loss* what to say. 我不知说什么好。 These mobile phones are *in great demand*. 这种手机需求量很大。 Keep *off the grass*. 请勿践踏草地。 They ran *out of coal*. 他们的煤用完了。 We must get *in touch with her*. 我们必须与她取得联系。 Soon he fell *in love with her*. 不久他爱上她了。
补语	I always find her *at her studies*. 我经常发现她在学习。 On the chair sat a young woman with a baby *in her arms*. 椅子上坐着一位年轻的妇女，怀里抱着一个婴儿。 I found him *in trouble*. 我发现他有麻烦了。 He imagined himself *on the point of death*. 他想象自己到了死亡的地步。 He didn't want me *in danger*. 他不想让我处于危险之中。
介词宾语	I saw her from *across the street*. 我从街对面望见了她。
同一短语不同作用	The doctors and the nurses *in the hospital* are very patient with the patients. 这家医院的大夫和护士对病人都很耐心。（作定语，修饰 the doctors and the nurses） Don't make noise *in the hospital*. 在医院里不要大声喧哗。（作地点状语，修饰谓语） She found herself *in the hospital* when she woke up. 她醒来时发现自己在医院里。（作宾补，补充说明宾语 herself） He is ill and has been *in the hospital* for a week. 他病了，已住院一星期。（用在系动词之后作表语）

Part 4 Unit Practice

1. Read aloud and write down the following words according to the phonics.

dialogue /science / sweetie /pioneer /radio /million /period / genius /fashion /experience

[ˈlaɪən] _____   [piːs] _____   [ˈdʒiːnɪəs] _____

[ˈmɑːrɪəʊ] _____   [ˈkwaɪət] _____   [ˈkʊki] _____

2. Put the school languages into English.

我要讲一个故事。   请跟我读。

看这幅图。   有问题请举手。

谁来试一下？   有人主动要做吗?

3. Put the following phrases into Chinese.

(1) classroom arrangement

(2) setting up the learning environment

(3) a place for the whole class to work together

(4) a place for students to work independently

(5) a place for teacher-directed small group work

(6) a rotation system or a self-selected system

(7) always model new activities

4. Read the compounding words and name them.

ten-year-old _____   sleeping-pills _____   quick-charge _____

takeaway _____   hand-made _____   world-famous _____

income _____   newborn _____   greenhouse _____

5. Decide the following sentences are true (T) or false (F).

(1) We got to the top of the mountain in daybreak. (   )

　　We got to the top of the mountain at daybreak. (   )

(2) By the end of next week, I will have finished this work. (   )

　　Till the end of next week, I will have finished this work. (   )

(3) We visited the old man on Sunday afternoon. (   )

　　We visited the old man in Sunday afternoon. (   )

(4) Do you know the girl in white? (   )

　　Do you know the girl on white? (   )

(5) There is a beautiful bird on the tree. (   )

　　There is a beautiful bird in the tree. (   )

(6) School will begin on September 1st. (   )

　　School will begin in September 1st. (   )

(7) There is an old stone bridge above the river. (   )

　　There is an old stone bridge over the river. (   )

(8) I haven't seen you during the summer holidays. (   )

   I haven't seen you since the beginning of the summer holidays. (   )

(9) On entering the classroom, I heard the good news. (   )

   At entering the classroom, I heard the good news. (   )

(10) At the beginning of the book, there are some interesting stories. (   )

   In the beginning of the book, there are some interesting stories. (   )

Part 5   Extended Reading

Outdoor Environment

The development of motor skills is essential to the total growth process of children. Current researches indicate that movement activates the brain and prepares it for learning. The outdoor environment is the natural place for this to occur. Carefully planning outdoor and motor activities is an opportune way to capitalize on children's natural motivation to move and learn.

Child Development

The Outdoor Environment offers experiences to facilitate growth and enhance skills in all areas of development.

Physical Skills: enhance large motor and eye-hand coordination, balance, strength, endurance and manipulation.

Social/Emotional Skills: nurture cooperation, negotiation, turn taking and role playing.

Language Skills: facilitate vocabulary development, positional words and conversational skills.

Intellectual Skills: reinforce sorting, classifying, creativity, imagination, problem solving, exploration, discovery, spatial relations and conversation through sand and water activities.

Suggested Outdoor Environment Materials

Slide (appropriate height)

Equipment for crawling and tunneling

Trucks and cars

Jump ropes

Pouring and scooping materials

Child-sized stilts

Impact material (pea gravel or sand)

Parachute

Games (ring toss or bean bags)

Climbing structure

Riding equipment

Push and pull toys

Walking path

Trash cans

Trees	Outdoor easels
Shady or partially covered play area	Tables and benches
Balls	Sand and water table
Binoculars	Science discovery tools
Sand toys	Garden and gardening tools
Assorted balls	First aid kit
Low balance beam	Sidewalk or hard, smooth surface
Hula hoops	Sidewalk chalk
Wagons	Dramatic play materials
Scooter boards	Buckets and paint brushes
Teeter totters	Line-up area

Arrangement

Arranging the outdoor environment is essential for effective planning. A well-planned play space maximizes the freedom of choice and independence of children. Teachers must continually assess the overall effectiveness of the outdoor area and make adjustments when and where needed. Many of the same considerations used in planning the indoor environment can be used when planning the outdoor environment.

- Space is large enough to accommodate the number of children and equipment.
- Children are easily supervised from any position.
- Sufficient equipment is available so children do not have to wait in line.
- A variety of age-appropriate materials and equipment are provided.
- A storage shed is available to store material and equipment.
- There is a balance of sunny and shady areas.
- There are clear pathways for running and riding toys.
- The play area is fenced and protected from traffic.
- Bathrooms and drinking fountains are easily accessible.
- Accommodations for the specific needs of each child are considered and addressed when appropriate.

Safety

Children are exuberant with their outdoor play, therefore planning for safety is critical. The best protection against injury is prevention. Include the following in your safety plan:

- Provide continuous supervision.
- Provide sufficient impact material under climbing equipment.
- Provide ample space around each piece of equipment.
- Maintain equipment regularly and report any equipment that is broken or unsafe.
- Select equipment and material that is appropriate for the child's intellectual, social / emotional, and physical development.
- Report accidents or hazardous situations to appropriate school staff immediately.
- Teach children the appropriate method for lining and exiting the playground quickly in the event of an emergency.

UNIT 6
Pre-school Music Education

> "Learning starts in infancy,
> long before
> formal education begins,
> and continues throughout life..."
>
> —Magda Gerber

Learning Objectives

Students will
- ★ review vowel digraph sounds
- ★ be familiar with school languages, chants, songs and stories
- ★ learn how to play a game for children
- ★ master new words and expressions
- ★ understand the musical developmental goals and learn how to help children synchronize their internal rhythm to an external input
- ★ review blending words and conjunctions

Part 1 Skills for Pre-school English Teaching

English Phonics V 自然拼读法（五）

Vowel Digraph Sounds (Part 3) 元音字母组合的读音 (3)

Vowel Digraph			Sounds & Examples		
			Long Vowel		Short Vowel
Oo	oa	[əu]	boat coat goal road		
	oi oy	[ɔi]	coin join noise toilet oil boy enjoy oyster toy		
	oo	[u:]	cool food moon school	[u]	book cook good look
	ou	[au] [u:]	about cloud house sound group soup rout through	[ʌ] [u]	country enough trouble should could would
	ow	[əu] [au]	blow grow low snow down flower now how		
Uu	ui	[u:]	bruise fruit juice recruit	[i]	build biscuit circuit guilt

Science Activities 科学活动

- Let's count the numbers: one, two, three ...
  我们来数数：一、二、三……
- How many colors do we have?
  有多少种颜色？
- How many toys are there?
  那里有多少个玩具？
- What's your answer?/ What's the number?
  答案是多少？/ 数字是多少？
- Which is more/bigger/smaller/longer/shorter?
  哪个比较多 / 比较大 / 比较小 / 比较长 / 比较短？

- Bring the long ones.
  把长的拿来。
- See, the bubble is getting bigger and bigger.
  看到没，泡泡越变越大。
- What's the shape?
  这是什么图形？
- What shape looks like a kite?
  什么形状像风筝？
- Whose school bag is heavier?
  谁的书包比较重？
- Who is taller, you or your friend?
  你跟你的朋友谁比较高？
- Can you paint it yellow /red /blue ...?
  你可以把它涂成黄色/红色/蓝色吗？
- What is the difference between an elephant and an ant?
  大象和蚂蚁有什么区别？

 Chants & Songs

What color is it? 它是什么颜色的?

Yellow! Yellow! What color is it?

It's yellow, it's yellow, it's a yellow hat.

Blue! Blue! What color is it?

It's blue, it's blue, it's a blue pencil.

Red! Red! What color is it?

It's red, it's red, it's a red bag.

Pink! Pink! What color is it?

It's pink, it's pink, it's a pink flower!

小小蜘蛛
Eensy Weensy Spider

Een-sy ween-sy spid-er went up the wa-ter spout, down came the rain and washed the spid-er out. Out came the sun and dried up all the rain, and the een-sy ween-sy spid-er went up the spout a-gain

一只小小蜘蛛慢慢爬上来，大雨落下把它冲跑了。太阳出来晒干瓦上雨，那只小小蜘蛛又慢慢爬上来。

Finger Plays 手指游戏：Itsy-Bitsy Spider

在美国，Itsy-Bitsy Spider 是一首非常流行的儿歌，几乎每个幼儿园的小朋友都会唱。这首歌叫做 Eensy Weensy Spider，英国人把它写作 Incy Wincy Spider，也可以说唱。

The Itsy-Bitsy spider（织织织织，小蜘蛛……）
先用左手的大拇指尖碰右手的中指尖，然后再用右手的大拇指尖碰左手的中指尖，双手交替，从中指到拇指，模仿蜘蛛走路的样子。

... went up the water spout.（……爬呀爬到水管上）
在做中指到拇指的动作时，一步一步把双手从下向上移动，好像蜘蛛往上爬一样。

Down came the rain ...（哗哗啦啦雨来啦……）
两手分开，往下落时张开手抖动手指，模仿下雨。

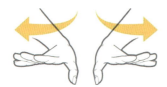

... and washed the spider out.（……蜘蛛蜘蛛冲走啦。）
停止做下雨的动作，双手分别向外拨，模仿雨水飞溅和流走的样子。

Out came the sun ...（红红太阳升上来……）
做完雨水冲走蜘蛛的动作立刻收回双手做成圆圈，然后双手上举，模仿冉冉升起的太阳。

... and dried up all the rain.（雨水雨水蒸干了。）
太阳升起来后，收回双手到刚才把蜘蛛冲走的动作，然后再把手朝内收回来，接着再双手上举，两手掌摊开，向外分，向上移动同时画小圈表示水蒸气的气泡。

And the itsy-bitsy spider ...（织织织织，小蜘蛛……）
重复第一步：先用左手大拇指碰右手的中指尖，再用右手的大拇指尖碰左手的中指尖，双手交替，从中指到拇指，模仿蜘蛛走路的样子。

... went up the spout again.（……再次呀爬到水管上。）
重复第二步：在做中指到拇指的动作时，双手从下向上移动，好像蜘蛛往上爬一样。

UNIT 6

Stories

Red Ball on the Floor 地上的红皮球

RED BALL ON THE FLOOR

The ball is on the floor. It is a red ball. It is a rubber ball. The baby looks at the ball. The cat looks at the ball. The cat is black. The cat walks over to the ball. The cat hits the ball with its paw. The ball rolls on the floor. The baby smiles.

Emily's Adventure 埃米莉历险记

Emily had a friend named Pipi. Pipi was a little dog. One day, Emily and Pipi went on a trip over the mountain and into the forest. They heard that there was delicious fresh fruit in the forest. They were walking along a path in the mountain when they came across a wolf. Emily got scared and hid behind a tree. Pipi was scared as well, but to protect Emily, he gathered his courage and barked loudly at the wolf. The wolf scared off. At last they arrived at the forest. Look at that! There was so much fruit! The fruit smelled like flowers. And the fresh apples were shiny and red. Emily saw Pipi looking up at the fruit. Pipi was too small and short to pick up an apple by himself, so Emily picked one for him. They sat and ate the yummy fruit together.

Game

Fishing 钓鱼

Objective: Listening

Aids: chopsticks, a magnet, strings, paperclips, flash cards, a timer

Rules 1. Tire a magnet to a chopstick to make a fishing pole; clip the paperclips onto flash cards; make two pools (circles with flash cards inside) on the floor.

2. Two teams compete. The teacher says "Catch the... ", and the children from both team take turns to come and fish up the right cards from the pool with the self-made pole, the faster one scores. The team that scores more wins.

Tips: Make sure that all the flash cards are dispersed and easy to fish up.

Part 2 Pre-school Education in English

Text

Pre-school Music Education

Movement Responses to Music

Movement responses to music is used in PME (Pre-school Music Education) to provide children with a useful tool to understand and sense the music through bodily movement. The songs presented in a lesson are virtually always accompanied by a motor action.

Movement responses to music can be regarded as a kinaesthetic representational way to internalise the music.

Movement activities become "aural counterparts", in which all aspects of sound: tone quality, duration, intensity, sounds and silences and timbre, can be experienced through the tension of muscles and energy input of the gestures. The experience of moving through space and time in itself can evoke implicit notions of close, far, up and down, high and low, consequently "organising incoming pitch-time phenomena" promoting the recall of musical aspects through movement. As a result, movement responses to music can be seen as an indicator of musical understanding in pre-school children.

Children can make movement responses to music because they possess a form of temporal representation. Representation of musical movement also implies the regulation of action in time, "synchronizing a motor action to an external rhythm", which is a crucial aspect of musical timing.

Pre-school Music Education

All PME activities are based on knowledge about the musical and general development of pre-school children. Enjoyment in the offered activities is an important aspect because the children will therefore be motivated to join in. According to Dewey however "Enjoyment on its own is not enough to make an experience educational". Although implicitly present, this is what distinguishes music courses from free musical play. An average PME course contains 10 lessons of 45 minutes every week with 8 to 10 participating children and their parents. During each lesson 10 to 12 activities will be offered. In each lesson only two new activities are presented because of the importance of repetition. Besides movements, often the songs involve the use of musical materials or a toy. When looking at musical development we can see that PME has a range of musical developmental goals: sense of rhythm: timing, reaction moment; sense of dynamics: loud and soft; sense of form: music versus no music (silence), variations; sense of tempo: fast and slow; voice formation: articulation, resonance; listening skills: attention, directing attention to a sound source. These musical developmental goals are supported by the motor activities accompanying each song. The movements themselves also portray the lyrics of the songs.

An example is "*Mommy Bear and Baby Bear*", a very steady paced activity.

Mommy Bear and Baby Bear

The children can walk on the beat of the song to let them experience the rhythm. After a few repetitions of the song, the tempo will be faster in order to let the children experience the difference between fast and slow. In the middle of the song, the children can lift a leg (portraying the lyrics), which is a reaction moment, a musical timing moment. The children need to pay attention to lift a leg at the right moment. The important thing is that they have to anticipate this moment. Therefore songs are repeated at least 5 times to give the children time to learn the song, to step into the movement and to synchronise their movements to the beat of the song. In this way, the children can build their memory; at a certain point they know what will come. Songs for children aged 0 to 4 in PME are short, only one verse. The longer the song, the more difficult it becomes to store all in memory and to anticipate the right moment to clap, stamp, and act. Hence imitation will take place. In this framework, it is important to distinguish timing—as in being on time—from imitation. In order to be on time you need to anticipate the moment. Imitation is responding to a stimulus but not anticipating that stimulus. Imitation therefore is always "too late". Stimulating movement responses is an important part of the musical developmental process: children are given the means and the time to synchronise their internal rhythm to an external input.

One, Two

In another example, *One, Two*, the children can experience, among others, through the use of musical material: wooden rhythm sticks, the sense of loud and soft and music versus no music. Here we will find the reaction moment at the end of the song: "and now we stop!". Guided experimentation time is often incorporated in this activity, making it possible for the children to express their own musical intentions. The PME teacher should observe closely and answer the children musically in the same manner as their performances. In this way the children themselves can initiate the movements and will find a confirmed response in the teacher's actions.

Notes

1. Background

In order to bring back singing into children's homes, Pre-school Music Education—the Dutch name for early childhood music education—created special courses for children aged 4 months to 4 years. The Pre-school Music Education (PME) courses have evolved from expert pedagogical practice over many years, but have not, so far, been subject to any kind of formal research.

为了把儿童的歌声带回家,"学前音乐教育"(儿童早期音乐教育的荷兰名字)为4个月到4岁的儿童开设了特别的课程。"学前音乐教育"(PME)课程已经从多年的专家教学实践中发展起来,但是到目前为止,还没有任何形式的正式研究。

This paper describes research, presently in progress, investigating movement responses to music of children aged 18 to 36 months in the PME environment. Taylor (1989) remarked "in music lessons with young children movement is often taken for granted". Fortunately movement responses to music by pre-school children are increasingly becoming the subject of research. However, the in-depth understanding of the movement responses of pre-school children is still in need of specific knowledge.

本文介绍了目前在PME环境中对18~36个月龄儿童的音乐运动反应的研究进展。泰勒(1989)说:"在音乐课上儿童做动作经常被认为是理所当然的。"幸运的是,学前儿童对音乐的运动反应越来越成为研究的对象。然而,对学前儿童运动反应的深入理解仍然需要专业知识。

2. Movement responses to music can be regarded as a kinaesthetic representational way to internalise the music.

音乐的运动反应可以看作是内化音乐的一种动感的表现方法。

3. Movement activities become "aural counterparts", in which all aspects of sound: tone quality, duration, intensity, sounds and silences and timbre, can be experienced through the tension of muscles and energy input of the gestures.

运动活动成为"副耳",使活动中声音的所有方面:音质、时长、强度、有声与无声及音色,都可以通过肌肉的张力和动作的能量输入来体验。

4. "organising incoming pitch-time phenomena" promoting the recall of musical aspects through movement.

"组织进入节拍时间现象",通过运动来促进对音乐方面的回忆。

5. "Enjoyment on its own is not enough to make an experience educational". Although implicitly present, this is what distinguishes music courses from free musical play.

"享受（乐趣）本身不足以让一段经历有教育意义。"尽管这是一种含蓄的表达，但这正是音乐课程与随便的音乐游戏的区别所在。

Structure：to make（动词）+ an experience（宾语）+ educational（宾补）

distinguish ... from：把……跟……区分开来，区分，识别

e.g. Can you distinguish right from wrong? 你能分清是非吗？

to distinguish good from evil 分清善恶

to distinguish reality from dreams 把现实与梦想区别开来

6. When looking at musical development we can see that PME has a range of musical developmental goals: sense of rhythm: timing, reaction moment; sense of dynamics: loud and soft; sense of form: music versus no music (silence), variations; sense of tempo: fast and slow; voice formation: articulation, resonance; listening skills: attention, directing attention to a sound source.

当关注音乐的发展时，我们可以看到，PME 的音乐发展目标是广泛的：节奏感：节拍点、反应点；强弱力度感：大、小声；曲式感：有音乐与无音乐(无声)，变奏；节拍感：快、慢；声音的形成：发声、共鸣；听音能力：专注，将注意力引向一个音源。

7. In the middle of the song the children can lift a leg—portraying the lyrics, which is a reaction moment: a musical timing moment. The children need to pay attention to lift a leg at the right moment.

歌曲的中间，儿童可以抬起一条腿（体现歌词内容），这是一个反应的时间点，即音乐的节拍点。儿童需要注意在恰当的时间点抬起一条腿。

8. In this framework it is important to distinguish timing—as in being on time—from imitation.

在这个框架中，区分节拍点（即踩准节拍点）和模仿是很重要的。

as in 正如，如同

e.g. As in all experimental sciences, we still do not know everything about nutrition.

就像所有实验科学一样，我们仍然没有完全认识营养作用。

9. The PME teacher should observe closely and answer the children musically in the same manner as their performances. In this way the children themselves can initiate the movements and will find a confirmed response in the teacher's actions.

学前音乐教育的老师应该密切观察并随着音乐以跟儿童同样的表演方式进行回应。这样，儿童自己就可以发起动作，并在老师的反应中找到肯定的答案。

Usefull Words and Expressions

virtually [ˈvəːtʃʊəli] *adv*. 事实上，几乎；实质上

accompany [əˈkʌmpəni] *vt*. 陪伴，伴随；伴奏

vi. 伴奏，伴唱

kinaesthetic [ˌkɪnɪsˈθetɪk] *adj*. [生理] 动觉的；（肌肉等）运动感觉的

representational [ˌreprɪzenˈteɪʃnl] *adj*. 代表的

internalise [inˈtəːnəlaɪz] *vt*. 主观化，内化

aural [ˈɔːrəl] *adj*. 听觉的；耳的；气味的；预兆的

counterpart [ˈkaʊntəpɑːt] *n*. 副本；配对物；相似物

tone [təʊn] *n*. 语气；色调；音调；音色

duration [djʊˈreɪʃn] *n.* 持续，持续的时间，时长
timbre [ˈtæmbə] *n.* 音色，音品
evoke [ɪˈvəʊk] *vt.* 唤起；产生，引起
implicit [ɪmˈplɪsɪt] *adj.* 不言明 [含蓄] 的；暗示的
implicitly [ɪmˈplɪsɪtli] *adv.* 含蓄地；隐式地
notion [ˈnəʊʃn] *n.* 概念；见解；打算
consequently [ˈkɒnsɪkwəntli] *adv.* 因此；终于
pitch [pɪtʃ] *n.* 音高；场地；最高点
pitch-time 间隔时间，节拍时间
phenomena [fəˈnɒmɪnə] *n.* 现象
　　　　（phenomenon 的复数）
recall [rɪˈkɔːl] *vt.* 召回；使想起，回想
　　　　n. 唤回；记忆力，回想
indicator [ˈɪndɪkeɪtə] *n.* 指示符；指针；迹象
possess [pəˈzes] *vt.* 拥有，掌握，懂得，具有
temporal [ˈtempərəl] *adj.* 时间的；暂存的
representation [ˌreprɪzenˈteɪʃn] *n.* 代表；象征
a form of temporal representation 一种时间的表现形式
regulation [ˌreɡjʊˈleɪʃn] *n.* 规则；管理；控制；规章
synchronise [ˈsɪŋkrənaɪz] *vt.* 校准时间，（使）同步
　　　　vi. （使）同步，（使）同速进行
crucial [ˈkruːʃəl] *adj.* 重要的；定局的
motivate [ˈməʊtɪveɪt] *vt.* 刺激；促动，激发
present [prɪˈzent] *vt.* 提出；介绍；呈现；赠送
　　　　[ˈpreznt] *adj.* 现在的；出席的
　　　　n. 现在；礼物
distinguish [dɪˈstɪŋɡwɪʃ] *vi.* & *vt.* 区分，辨别，识别

participate [pɑːˈtɪsɪpeɪt] *vi.* & *vt.* 参与，参加
repetition [ˌrepəˈtɪʃn] *n.* 重复；[乐]复唱，复奏
rhythm [ˈrɪðəm] *n.* [诗]节奏，韵律，[乐]节拍
dynamics [daɪˈnæmɪks] *n.* （音乐中的）力度变化
versus [ˈvɜːsəs] *prep.* 对；与……相对；对抗
variation [ˌveərɪˈeɪʃn] *n.* 变化；变奏曲；变量
tempo [ˈtempəʊ] *n.* [乐]速度，拍子
articulation [ɑːˌtɪkjʊˈleɪʃn] *n.* 发音；清晰度；咬合
resonance [ˈrezənəns] *n.* 共振；共鸣；反响
portray [pɔːˈtreɪ] *vt.* 描绘；描述；画像；描画
lyrics [ˈlɪrɪks] *adj.* 抒情的；吟唱的
　　　　n. 抒情诗；歌词
pace [peɪs] *n.* 一步；长度单位；步幅；步调；快步
　　　　vt. 步测；调整步调；训练马溜蹄
steady paced 节奏稳定的
beat [biːt] *n.* 拍子；敲击；有规律的一连串敲打
anticipate [ænˈtɪsɪpeɪt] *vt.* 预期，期望，抢先
verse [vɜːs] *n.* 诗；诗篇；韵文；诗节
hence [hens] *adv.* 从此；因此，所以；于是；今后
stimulus [ˈstɪmjʊləs] *n.* 刺激；激励；刺激物
　　　　（复数 stimuluses 或 stimuli）
internal [ɪnˈtɜːnl] *adj.* 内部的；体内的；内心的
external [ɪkˈstɜːnl] *adj.* 外部的；表面上的
input [ˈɪnpʊt] *n.* 输入，投入
wooden rhythm stick 木制节奏棒
incorporate [ɪnˈkɔːpəreɪt] *vt.* 包含；吸收；体现
　　　　vi. 合并；混合

Ideological and Political Concept

　　学前音乐教育为儿童提供了一种通过身体动作来理解和感知音乐的有用工具，也是学前儿童音乐理解力的指标。音乐教育的实践活动能够使儿童获得音乐艺术内涵的教育，与此同时培养儿童的审美情趣、塑造儿童良好的个性及创造力。在音乐及其他艺术形式的教育活动设计中，幼教工作者应注重中华文明和文化素养教育的渗透，培养文化认同感、树立文化自信心。

Part 3 English Proficiency

Word Building VI 构词（六）

Blending—混合法

1. 混合法定义

> Blending is the formation of new words by combining parts of two words or a word plus a part of another word.
>
> 混合法（混成法、拼缀法）是将两个词混搭在一起，其中至少一个词失去部分音节或字母，新词的意义是组混新词的融合或叠加。

2. 混合法分类

(1) the first part of the first word + the last part of the second word：
取第一个词的首部接第二个词的尾部：

motel (**mo**tor + ho**tel**) 汽车旅馆 **tele**cast (**tele**vision + broad**cast**) 电视广播
Chunnel (**ch**annel + t**unnel**) 海峡隧道 **sm**og (**sm**oke + f**og**) 烟雾
brunch (**br**eakfast + l**unch**) 早午餐 **b**it (**b**inary dig**it**) 位元（二进制中的一单位）

(2) the whole part of the first word + the last part of the second word：
保持第一个词的原形，取第二个词的尾部：

lunarnaut (**lunar** + astro**naut**) 登月宇航员 **air**tel (**air** + ho**tel**) 机场宾馆
newscast (**news** + broad**cast**) 新闻报道 **fact**ion (**fact** + fict**ion**) 纪实文学
travelogue (**travel** + cata**logue**) 旅行见闻讲座 **slim**nastics (**slim** + gym**nastics**) 减肥体操

(3) the first part of the first word + the whole part of the second word：
取第一个词的首部，保持第二个词的原形：

Eurasian (**Eur**ope + **Asian**) 欧亚混血儿 **heli**pad (**heli**copter + **pad**) 直升机升降场
paratroops (**para**chute + **troops**) 空降部队 **psy**warrior (**psy**chological + **warrior**) 心理战专家
docudrama (**docu**ment + **drama**) 纪录片 **tele**diagnosis (**tele**vision + **diagnosis**) 远距侦探
medicare (**medi**cal + **care**) 医疗照顾方案 **auto**camp (**auto**mobile + **camp**) 汽车露营

(4) the first part of the first word + the first part of the second word:
取第一个词和第二个词的首部：

interpol (**inter**national **pol**ice) 国际警察 **mo**ped (**mo**tor **ped**al-cycle) 轻型脚踏摩托车
comsat (**com**munications + **sat**ellite) 通信卫星 **sit**com (**sit**uation + **com**edy) 情景喜剧
comint (**com**munications + **int**elligence) 通信情报 **sci-fi** (**sci**ence + **fi**ction) 科幻小说

Conjunction 连词

英语连词是一种虚词，用于连接单词、短语、从句或句子，在句子中不单独用作句子成分。连词按其性质可分为并列连词和从属连词。

1. 并列连词的用法

并列连词用于连接并列的单词、短语或句子。

平行对等
- When he returned, she *and* Simon had already gone. 他回来时，她和西蒙已经走了。
- Both New York *and* London have traffic problems. 纽约和伦敦都存在交通问题。
- It is important for you *as well as* for me. 这对你和对我来说，都很重要。
- The weather is mild today; it is *neither* cold *nor* hot. 今天天气很温暖，不冷也不热。
- Things here are *not only* inexpensive *but also* of good quality. 这儿的东西又便宜又好。

转折
- I don't want to leave, *but* I can't go on. 我不想离开，但我继续不下去了。
- I don't eat much, *yet* I am a size 16. 我吃得并不多，但是却穿16码的衣服。
- The news may be unexpected; *nevertheless*, it is true. 这消息可能是出乎意料的，然而是真实的。
- The walls are green, *while* the ceiling is white. 墙是绿色的，而天花板是白色的。

选择
- The man was a fool, he thought, *or* at least incompetent.
  他想，那人是个傻瓜，或者说，至少很无能。
- He must be *either* mad *or* drunk. 他要么是疯了，要么是喝醉了。
- *Either* Tom *or* I am to be blame. 该受责备的，不是汤姆就是我。

因果
- The child had a bad cough, *so* his mother took him to the doctor.
  这孩子咳得很厉害，所以他妈妈带他去看医生。
- *Because* it is an area of outstanding natural beauty, you can't build on it.
  考虑到这一带自然风光旖旎，你不能建在这里。
- You are supposed to get rid of carelessness, *for* it often leads to serious errors.
  你们一定要克服粗枝大叶，因为粗枝大叶常常引起严重的错误。(for 句不能在前)

递进
- I'm sure we watched the nightly news, *and then* we turned on the movie.
  我肯定我们是先看了晚间新闻，然后才开始看的电影。
- I don't want to go there; *furthermore*, I have no time to do so.
  我不想去那里，而且我也没时间去。

2. 从属连词的用法

从属连词主要引出名词性从句（主语从句、宾语从句、表语从句等）和状语从句（时间状语从句、条件状语从句、目的状语从句等）。

（1）that 引导的名词性从句。

That our team had won the game was good news to us. 我们队赢了这场比赛对我们来说是个好消息。 It is certain *that* he will do well in his new job. 他一定会在新工作中表现出色。	主语 真主语
Everybody knows (*that*) the earth goes round the sun. 人人都知道地球绕着太阳转。 He has made it clear *that* he will not give in. 他已明确表示不会让步。 Your homework is quite good except *that* you have made two small mistakes. 你的作业很好，只是你犯了两个小错误。	宾语 真宾语 介词宾语
My decision is *that* we are to start at 6 tomorrow morning. 我的决定是明天早上 6 点开始。 My advice is *that* you must give up smoking right now. 我的建议是你现在必须戒烟。	表语
The news *that* our team had won the game excited everybody. 我们队赢了比赛的消息使大家都很兴奋。 The fact *that* he is a thief shocked all of us. 他是小偷的事实震惊了我们所有人。	同位语

（2）whether / if（是否）引导的名词性从句。

主语	*Whether* the work can be completed on time is doubtful. 这项工作能否按时完成是值得怀疑的。 It is doubtful *whether / if* the work can be completed on time.（if 从句不能在前） 这项工作能否按时完成还值得怀疑。
宾语	I don't care *whether / if* he comes. 我不在乎他是否来。 I don't care *whether or not* he comes.（不能用 if 跟 or not）我不在乎他是否来。
表语	The problem is *whether* the money will be enough.（不用 if） 他的问题是钱是否足够。
同位语	I have no idea *whether* the money will be enough.（不用 if） 我不知道这些钱是否够用。

（3）连接代词引导的名词性从句。

What they need is a good rest. 他们需要的是好好休息。（主语从句）

Whoever did this job must be rewarded. 无论谁做这项工作都必须得到奖励。（主语从句）

Whichever he likes will be given to him. 他喜欢哪个就给他。（主语从句）

It hasn't been decided *who* will manage the company. 谁来管理公司还没有决定。（真主语从句）

They haven't decided *whom* they should help. 他们还没有决定应该帮助谁。（宾语从句）

We shall not forget *when* the meeting will be held. （宾语从句）

She walked up to *where* he stood. 她走到他所站的地方。（介宾从句）

I can judge by *what* I know of him. 我可以根据我对他的了解来判断。（介宾从句）

（4）连接副词引导的名词性从句和状语从句。

I can't imagine *how* he did it. 我无法想象他是怎么做到的。（宾语从句）

It looks/seems *as if* it's going to rain. 看起来好像要下雨了。（表语从句）

When they got there, the train has left. 当他们到达那里时，火车已经开走了。（时间状语从句）

Since you have no spirit, I have to settle for beer.
既然你没烈酒，我就将就喝点啤酒吧。（原因状语从句）

He was in love with her, *although* he did not put that name to it.
他爱着她，虽然他没有将其称为爱。（让步状语从句）

Let me remind you once again so *that* you won't forget.
我再说一遍，省得你忘了。（目的状语从句）

This story is *so* interesting *that* I want to read it again.
这个故事如此有趣以至我想再读一遍。（结果状语从句）

He'll never pay up *unless* you get tough with him.
你如果不对他硬点，他是绝不会把钱付清的。（条件状语从句）

As long as we are united, there is no difficulty we cannot overcome.
只要大伙儿团结一心，就没有克服不了的困难。（条件状语从句）

Part 4　Unit Practice

1. Read aloud and write down the following words according to the phonics.

goal / noise / moon / soup / grow / juice / cook / enough / biscuit / sound

[bəʊt] _____　　　　[dʒɔɪn] _____　　　　[fru:t] _____

[bləʊ] _____　　　　[fu:d] _____　　　　　[haʊs] _____

2. Put the school languages into English.

你有几个玩具？　　　　　　什么形状像风筝？

谁的书包比较重？　　　　　把这个圆形涂成蓝色。

把长的铅笔拿过来。　　　　苹果和香蕉有什么不同？

3. Put the following phrases into Chinese.

（1）Pre-school children Music Education

（2）movement responses to music

（3）understand and sense the music through bodily movement

（4）motor activities accompanying each song

（5）stimulating movement responses

4. Read the blending words and name them.

telecast _____   cheeseburger _____   slimnastics _____
psywarrior _____   interpol _____   motorcamp _____
smog _____   motel _____   sitcom _____

5. Complete the short passage by filling conjunctions in the blanks.

One day I was playing the piano（1）_____ I heard a knock at the door. It was my neighbour Jack. He wanted to buy a second-hand piano. Everyone said I played piano well,（2）_____ he asked me for help to judge the tone of the piano. We arrived at the owner's house and I looked the piano over,（3）_____ sat down and played a mixture of honky-tonk numbers（4）_____ classical pieces. When I finished, I said that the wood was rotten, but（5）_____ the sound was good and（6）_____ he should buy it.

Part 5 Extended Reading

Music and Movement Center

Music delights young children and invites them to participate. A well-equipped Music and Movement Center is a place where young children experiment with sounds while they create their own music. They gain an appreciation and love of music that will bring them enjoyment for years to come.

Child Development

The Music and Movement Center offers many experiences to facilitate growth and enhance skills in all areas of development.

Physical Skills: enhance fine and gross motor skills, develop rhythm, balance, and spatial awareness.

Social/Emotional Skills: provide a means to express feelings and emotions, enhance self-concept, promote cooperation and working with others, and induces feelings of calm and relaxation.

Language Skills: increase oral communication skills, vocabulary growth and listening skills; develop an appreciation for poetry and rhyme, and increase auditory discrimination skills.

Intellectual Skills: develop creativity and imagination, promote problem solving skills, enhance concept development, and encourage exploration and promote discovery.

Points to Remember

• Music can set the tone for the classroom. Soft music calms a busy room whereas loud or fast music

stimulates the students.
- Music can activate the brain. Learning set to music, like the "ABC" song, embeds learning more quickly and on a deeper level.
- Music is effective during transition times such as clean-up, calming down for a story or rest, or getting ready to begin or end the day. Do not limit music experiences to just center time.
- Music can be a tool of classroom management. Singing can often attract a child's attention while a speaking voice cannot. Include classroom transition songs on charts for students to sing along with at center time.
- Music can be experienced and enjoyed by a whole group during circle time, in small groups and individually.
- Use a voice range for singing that is comfortable for children.
- Let music be spontaneous, planned or an outgrowth of another activity.
- Music can be used to create appreciation of other cultures.

Suggested Music and Movement Materials

CD player and CDs

Rhythm sticks
Scarves
Radio
Books that are songs
Toy or real microphones
Charts with favorite songs
Cassette recorder, cassettes, and blank tapes
Drums
Bells
Cymbals
Piano
Song-based books
Shakers
Mirrors
Area rug
Multicultural musical instruments
Piano music
Staff paper
Costumes
Guitar
Recorders
Sanitizing supplies
Posters of bands and orchestras
Dance rug
Ballet shoes
Hats

Large ball
Keyboard
Materials for creating instruments
Shelves
Tubs with labels
Exercise chart
Exercise mat
Rebus exercise cards
Work out props
Exercise records, tapes, and videos
Books
Journals
Plain paper
Writing utensils
Dance costumes
Maracas
Sand blocks
Chimes
Triangles
Television
Video player
Finger cymbals
Xylophone
Tap shoes
Canes

Language Development

> "Each time one prematurely teaches a child something he could have discovered for himself, that child is kept from inventing it and consequently from understanding it completely."
>
> —Jean Piaget

Learning Objectives

Students will
- ★ review English phonics: r-team sounds
- ★ be familiar with school languages, chants, songs and stories
- ★ learn how to play a game for children
- ★ master new words and expressions
- ★ understand the importance of oral language syntax for beginning reading and learn how to develop children's early literacy ability
- ★ review clipping words, infinitives and gerunds

Part 1　Skills for Pre-school English Teaching

English Phonics VI 自然拼读法（六）

R-team Sounds 辅音字母组合的读音

Phonics		Examples	Phonics		Examples
ar	[ɑː]	car　star　park　market	air are	[eə]	air　chair　hair　pair
	[ə]	dollar　popular　sugar			bare　care　dare　hare
er	[əː]	certain　her　person　term	eer	[ɪə]	beer　cheer　deer　peer
	[ə]	teacher　farmer　cover			dear　hear　near　tear (n.)
ir	[əː]	bird　circle　dirty　first girl　shirt　skirt　third	ear	[əː]	earn　heard　learn　early
				[eə]	bear　pear　tear (v.)　wear
ur	[əː]	hurt　nurse　purple　turn	ire	[aɪə]	fire　tire　desire　hire
or	[ɔː]	horse　morning　north short　support　torch	oor ore	[ɔː]	door　floor　moor　poor core　gore　more　store
	[əː]	work　word　world　worse	our		four　source　pour　your
	[ə]	actor　doctor　Professor		[auə]	our　hour　flour　sour

Art Activities 美术活动

- You're going to get a piece of paper.
  你们要拿到一张纸。
- Let's start! / Here we go!
  开始吧！
- Fold it in half and open it again.
  把它对折，然后打开。
- Now turn the paper over.
  现在把纸翻过来。

- Let me see, what color do you like?
  让我看看，你们喜欢什么颜色？
- Would you like painting / drawing?
  你喜欢画画吗？
- What's your favorite color?
  你最喜欢什么颜色？
- I'm going to draw an apple.
  我要画一个苹果。
- You can watch. /Watch, first.
  你们可以先看。
- Can you pass me that piece of paper?
  可以递给我那张纸吗？
- Yes. Here you are.
  可以，给你。
- Put away your pencils/brushes.
  把你的笔放回去。
- Take the scissors to cut the lid off.
  用剪刀把盖子剪下来。
- Finish your painting/drawing.
  把画画完。
- Put your name on your painting/drawing.
  在画上写上你的名字。

 Chants & Songs

Color This Clown 给小丑涂颜色

Color this clown, up and down,

Hands pink, ears brown.

Face white, eyes blue,

Hair red, mouth too.

Nose purple, feet grey,

Body orange, hip hooray!

Legs black, car yellow,

Happy, happy, fellow!

OLD MACDONALD HAD A FARM
(Song for Children)

1 = G 4/4

| 1 1 1 1 | 6 6 5 — | 3 3 2 2 |
1~6. Old Mac-don-ald had a farm, E, I, E, I,

| 1 — 5 | 1 1 1 1 | 6 6 5 — |
O.　　　And on that farm he had some DUCKS,
O.　　　And on that farm he had some COWS,
O.　　　And on that farm he had some HORSES,
O.　　　And on that farm he had some CHICKENS,
O.　　　And on that farm he had some PIGS,
O.　　　And on that farm he had some DOGS,

| 3 3 2 2 | 1 — 5 5 | 1 1 1 5 5 |
E, I, E, I, O. With a quack-quack here and a
E, I, E, I, O. With a moo-moo here and a
E, I, E, I, O. With a neigh-neigh here and a
E, I, E, I, O. With a cluck-cluck here and a
E, I, E, I, O. With a oink-oink here and a
E, I, E, I, O. With a woof-woof here and a

| 1 1 1 — | 1 1 1 1 | 1 1 1 |
quack-quack there.　Here a quack, there a quack,
moo-moo there.　Here a moo, there a moo,
neigh-neigh there.　Here a neigh, there a neigh,
cluck-cluck there.　Here a cluck, there a cluck,
oink-oink there.　Here a oink, there a oink,
woof-woof there.　Here a woo, there a woof,

| 1 1 1 1 | 1 1 | 1 1 1 1 |
ev- ery where a quack-quack. Old Mac- don- ald
ev- ery where a moo-moo. Old Mac- don- ald
ev- ery where a neigh-neigh. Old Mac- don- ald
ev- ery where a cluck-cluck. Old Mac- don- ald
ev- ery where a oink-oink. Old Mac- don- ald
ev- ery where a woof-woof. Old Mac- don- ald

| 6 6 5 — | 3 3 2 2 | 1 — — 0 ‖
had a farm,　　　E, I, E, I, O.

《老麦克唐纳有一个农场》是一首少年儿童歌曲，可用来练习一些动物的拟声词。歌词大意：

老麦克唐纳有一个农场，农场里一些鸭子。鸭子这里嘎嘎叫一下，那里叫一下，农场到处是嘎嘎声。

注：moo-moo　　　是牛的叫声。
　　neigh-neigh　是马的叫声。
　　cluck-cluck　是鸡的叫声。
　　oink-oink,　　是猪的叫声。
　　woof-woof　　是狗的叫声。
　　Macdonald　　人名

 Stories

Where is Tobi 托比在哪里

Tobi hasn't eaten his dinner. Where is he? Is he behind the door? Is he inside the clock? Is he under the stairs? Is he in the closet? There is Tobi! He is under the rug.

My Vacation 我的假期

"I'm going vacation! I'm going to the beach," I said to Jimmy. "I'm going vacation! I'm going to the mountains," Jimmy said. "Beaches are fun," I said to Jimmy. "No, mountains are fun," Jimmy said. I wanted to show him how much fun the beaches are. I decided to send him the postcards. "Today is Monday. It is very funny today. I have to put on sun block," I wrote. But it was very windy and cold. "Today is Tuesday. I found pretty seashells in the sand," I wrote. But I couldn't find anything except seaweed. "Today is Wednesday. I played in the sand. The whether is beautiful," I wrote. But it was raining all day. "Today is Thursday. I built a sand castle. It looked great!" I wrote. But I couldn't build anything because of the waves. "Today is Friday. I love swimming in the ocean," I wrote. But I don't know how to swim. "Today is Saturday. I love playing in the waves," I wrote. But I couldn't go in the water. The waves were too high. "Today is Sunday. I'm going home today. I had so much fun," I wrote. But I didn't.

UNIT 7

Lip-reading 读唇语

Objective: mastering the pronunciation of words / speeches

Rules: The teacher will mouth a word / sentence which children learnt. children lip-read the sound of the word / sentence in mind by watching the way the teacher's lips move, and then shout it out correctly. The fastest child wins.

Tips: The teacher may exaggerate the lips movement and the facial expression to make the game easier and more interesting.

Language: Please watch the way my lips move carefully. I will just mouth a word /sentence without sound. As long as you guess it, shout it out loud as quickly as you can. If that's it, you'll get a Good Job Sticker. Furthermore, once you're the fastest, you'll win the first prize.

Ippo Oppo 反着来

Objective: Practicing words with opposite meanings

Rules: Name two puppets "Ippo" and "Oppo". Oppo always says the opposite of what Ippo says, such as if Ippo says "good", Oppo must say "bad". Point one child "Ippo", and another one "Oppo" to play the game.

Tips: The teacher may put some flash / picture cards around the classroom for the children's references; the teacher had better join the game.

Samples: good/bad; big/small; happy/sad; much/little; left/ right; black/ white; in/out; up/down; fast/slow; come/go; yes/no; day/night; long/short; hard/soft; heavy/light...

Part 2 Pre-school Education in English

Language Development

Oral Language and Written Language

Oral language is all around us and we take it for granted, unaware of the choices we make or the form of language we use. However, when writing, written language demands that there is conscious attention to form and this involves choices to do with semantics, syntax and phonology. For example, a four-year-old beginning invented speller who wants to write "I have a chair" has to consider the word order and meanings and when he writes the word "chair", the child needs to pay attention to phonemes in a way that he never had to when learning to speak. The importance of phonological awareness cannot be underestimated and Richgels (2004) points out that children are born to perceive phonemes. For example, from birth they can perceive the difference between /s/ and /z/. Richgels (2004) also writes that in the study of oral language the greatest attention in research has been on phonology, and even then, mostly on a subset of phonological knowledge; the awareness of phonemes.

The syntax of oral language has been identified as important for beginning reading. It is argued that children with a high competence in oral language sentence construction bring rich language to the new task of reading and writing. The Record of Oral Language (ROL), (Clay et al. 2007) was developed to measure children's syntax. However many of the sentences in the ROL have a structure, and the structure is similar to written language which uses more complex embedded syntax structures. In contrast to written language, the syntactic structure of oral language is more likely to be fragmented with clauses and phrases strung together, false starts and repetitions and abandoned intonation units. For example it is obvious there is a difference between oral and written language syntax when comparing an oral speech with a written statement which is read aloud.

A child's oral vocabulary development is one of the most visible and important aspects of language acquisition in children. The number of words in a child's vocabulary is an indicator of his or her linguistic health and a factor in his or her ability to use language in varied contexts and for multiple purposes. The everyday spoken language that children hear has fewer rare words compared to the rare words that occur in books read aloud.

With oral language vocabulary noted as an important link in learning to read it was assumed in this research that a child's vocabulary would neatly link to their reading proficiency. The children who had a rich vocabulary were assumed to be the more effective readers.

Discussion: Disconnections between oral language and learning to read

This small study of a group of twenty-three children beginning school reveals that the steps from oral language to early reading is not a neat hierarchical step-by-step process for many children. The study raises many questions. How is it that children with low scores on oral language receptive vocabulary can be relatively advanced readers in the first year of school? Why are children who have high oral language scores not also advanced readers? Why are some children low on all counts of oral language and reading?

One explanation for this is that oral language is not the same as written language. Oral language and written language have different vocabulary, syntax and mechanics of representation. The vocabulary, syntax and mechanics of representation in oral language and written language will now be contrasted.

Table 1 Oral Language and Written Language Vocabulary

Oral Language	Written Language
Sit over there.	Tom sat on the chair.
Oral language is contextual and relies on gestures and is often a sentence fragment. In written language the subject and the object are identified.	

In oral language, meanings can be expressed through gestures, facial expressions and intonations and the articulation of nouns may not be essential. However in written language, meanings must be accomplished through the use of explicit language and the grammatical use of the subject and the object occurs in sentences. In oral language, a sentence fragment may be "Sit over there." with a gesture. In the written language sentence "Tom sat on the chair." the subject "Tom" is identified as well as the object "chair."

Regarding vocabulary there are more rare words in written language than spoken language. As an example, the picture book *Where the wild things are* contains rare words such as "gnashing teeth" and "terrible roars" which may not occur in everyday conversation. In an analysis of a range of spoken and written texts, Hayes and Ahrens (1988) revealed the amount of rare words used in everyday speech to be 17.3 in one thousand words whereas in children's books there were 30.9 rare words per one thousand words, nearly double the amount in everyday speech. It is probable that children who experience being read to before school will be exposed to more rare words and increase their vocabulary more so than children who do not experience shared book reading at home. Regarding the issue of whether oral language is mapped to written language, it is more likely that written language provides models of syntax and vocabulary which then become used in oral language.

Table 2 Oral Language and Written Language Sentence Structures

Oral Language	Written Language
We walked for charity on Sunday.	The Charity Walk will raise money on Sunday.
Nominalisation occurs where a verb is changed to a noun.	
We hid the book.	The book was hidden.
Objects are placed first in a sentence in written language.	
That cat chased a bird.	The cat from next door was chasing a bird.
In written language there is an increased number of lexical items such as nouns, adjectives, verbs and adverbs in a sentence.	

The syntax of written language is different from that of oral language. For example in the book *Where the wild things are* we read about Max who "sailed off through night and day and in and out of weeks" which is a lyrical use of language with many lexical items. The syntax of written language contains more embedded clauses, direct speech, saying verbs and in the following example the subject Max, occurs part way through the sentence "And now," cried Max, "let the wild rumpus start!"

The example above "The cat from next door was chasing a bird" is from the Record of oral language (Clay et al. 2007) and it is an example of more complex sentences which is more similar to written language syntax than the syntax of spoken language.

Table 3　Oral Language and Written Language Reference Conventions or Mechanics

Oral Language	Written Language
sounds	letters
intonation, stress, pitch	punctuation and capital letters, underline and bold font
expressions to indicate topic changes, "now, right, right then"	headings, new pages, paragraphs, sections or chapters, words like "first, second, summary"

Written language contains letters to represent sounds, punctuation and various font styles to represent intonation, stress and pitch. The sections or new ideas are represented in written language with headings, paragraphs and words to show the sequence of ideas, for example first, second, last and summary.

Notes

1. Background

This text is an excerpt from *Oral language and beginning reading: Exploring connections and disconnections*, a study report by Susan Hill, Associate Professor in Early Childhood Education, University of South Australia. The purpose of the study was to explore the connections between young children's oral language vocabulary and children's reading of written language in beginning reading books. Oral language has been viewed as the foundation for emergent reading development as it provides the semantic base, syntactic base and phonological base for successfully moving from oral to written language. In fact in the years before school the development of children's oral language in the home environment is viewed as an important factor for early reading success.

本文节选自南澳大利亚大学儿童早期教育副教授苏珊·希尔的研究报告《口头语言和开始阅读：探索关联与无关》。该研究旨在探讨幼儿口语词汇与幼儿阅读书面语的关系。口语是早期阅读发展的基础，它为从口语到书面语的成功提供了语义基础、句法基础和语音基础。事实上，在学龄前，儿童在家庭环境中的口头语言的发展被看作是早期阅读成功的一个重要因素。

2. Oral language is all around us and we take it for granted, unaware of the choices we make or the form of language we use.

口头语言就在我们周围，我们认为它是理所当然的，没有意识到我们做出的选择或我们使用语言的形式。

take for granted 认为……理所当然，想当然

e.g. We take for granted the things that we should be giving thanks for.

我们通常把我们应该感谢的事视为理所当然。

unaware of 没觉察到，没有意识到

e.g. Many people are unaware of just how much food and drink they consume.

许多人并不知道他们究竟消耗掉了多少食品和饮料。

3. ... and this involves choices to do with semantics, syntax and phonology. 这涉及与语义、句法和语音有关的选择。

to do with... 不定式短语作后置定语，修饰 choices，意为"有关"。

e.g. This has nothing to do with you. 这与你不相干。

4. For example, a four-year-old beginning invented speller who wants to write "I have a chair" has to consider the word order and meanings and when he writes the word "chair", the child needs to pay attention to phonemes in a way that he never had to when learning to speak.

例如，一个四岁的开始模拟拼写的幼儿想要写"我有一把椅子"，他必须考虑单词的顺序和含义，当他写"椅子"这个单词时，还需要注意音素，这是他在学习说话时从来没有的。

句子结构分析：这是一个由 and 连接的并列复合句；

前句：主语 a ... speller + 定语从句 who ... a chair + 谓语 has to ... meanings

后句：时间状语 when ... chair + 主语 the child+ 谓语 needs to ... phonemes

　　　　+ 方式状语部分 in a way + 定语从句 they ... to (+ 状语 when ... speak)

5. It is argued that children with a high competence in oral language sentence construction bring rich language to the new task of reading and writing.

有人认为，口语句子建构能力较强的幼儿能为阅读和写作这种新任务带来丰富的语言。

句子结构分析：it 是形式主语；that 引导真主语从句

主语从句中：主语部分 children+ 后置定语 with ... construction, + 谓语部分 bring ... writing

6. In contrast to written language, the syntactic structure of oral language is more likely to be fragmented with clauses and phrases strung together, false starts and repetitions and abandoned intonation units.

与书面语言不同的是，口语的句法结构更可能是支离破碎的从句和短语串在一起，错误的开头，重复和随意的调群。

in contrast to 与……对比（或对照）；与……相反

e.g. In contrast to the previous year, the situation is much better now.

与前一年相比，现在情况已经好多了。

be likely to 倾向于，很有可能

e.g. We'll be likely to hire several people this month. 这个月我们很有可能雇佣一些人。

7. For example it is obvious there is a difference between oral and written language syntax when comparing an oral speech with a written statement which is read aloud.

例如，当一段口语表达与一段朗读出来的书面语表达进行对比时，口语和书面语的区别是明显的。

句子结构分析：it 是形式主语，there is ... aloud 是真正的主语从句；

真主语从句中 which is read aloud 是定语从句，修饰 a written statement。

compare ... with ... 把……和……比较（常表示同类相比，比较）
e.g. Let's compare this article with that one. 让我们把这篇文章和那篇文章作一下比较。
compare ... to ... 把……比作……（常表示异类相比，比喻）
e.g. The heart is often compared to a pump. 心脏常被比作水泵。

8. With oral language vocabulary noted as an important link in learning to read it was assumed in this research that a child's vocabulary would neatly link to their reading proficiency.
因为口语词汇被认为与学习阅读有重要关联，本研究假定儿童的词汇量与阅读水平有着密切的联系。
(be) noted as 被注明为；以……而闻名
e.g. Suppose a word belongs to the functional categories, its lexical semantic feature can be noted as [-N,-V].
如果一个词是功能语类，它的语类特征就都可以描写为 [-N,-V]。
It is assumed that... 人们认为；据推测；假定
e.g. It is assumed that you already have such test cases in order to run this step.
我们假定您已经获得了运行此步骤所需的此类测试用例。

9. How is it that children with low scores on oral language receptive vocabulary can be relatively advanced readers in the first year of school?
为什么在口语表达能力方面得分较低的儿童，在上学后的第一年里成为相对高水平的阅读者呢？
How is it that... 为什么
e.g. How is it that you are still here? 你为什么还在这儿？
advanced reader 高水平的阅读者

10. Why are some children low on all counts of oral language and reading? 为什么有些儿童的口语和阅读能力都很低呢？
on all counts 在各方面；完全；在所有项
e.g. He was cleared on all counts of complicity to slander, dealing in stolen property and breach of trust.
他同时也澄清了所有同谋指控，包括诽谤、交易失窃财产和背信罪。

11. It is probable that children who experience being read to before school will be exposed to more rare words and increase their vocabulary more so than children who do not experience shared book reading at home.
很有可能，那些在上学之前家长给他们朗读过书的儿童会接触到更多的生僻词，所以比那些在家里没有听人朗读过书的儿童增加更多词汇量。
being read to 动名词短语的被动式，作定语从句谓语动词 experience 的宾语。
在此句中，意为"听别人为自己朗读"。
more so than 比……多
e.g. She had always been silent and thoughtful, and now she was more so than ever.
她一直就是一个沉静和深思的孩子，现在她变得更是这样了。

Useful Words & Expressions

unaware [ˌʌnəˈweə] *adj.* 不知道的，无意的
　　　　　　　　　adv. 意外地；不知不觉地
conscious [ˈkɒnʃəs] *adj.* 意识到的；故意的

semantics [sɪˈmæntɪks] *n.* [语] 语义学；语义论
syntax [ˈsɪntæks] *n.* 语法；句法；句法规则
phonology [fəˈnɒlədʒɪ] *n.* 音系学；音韵学

UNIT 7

phonological [ˌfəʊnəˈlɒdʒɪkəl] *adj.* 音韵学的
perceive [pəˈsiːv] *v.* 理解；意识到；察觉，发觉
subset [ˈsʌbset] *n.* 子集
argue [ˈɑːgjuː] *vi.* 争论，辩论；提出理由
　　　　　　　vt. 辩论，争论；证明；说服
competence [ˈkɒmpɪtəns] *n.* 能力；技能；胜任
complex [ˈkɒmpleks] *adj.* 复杂的，难懂的
embed [ɪmˈbed] *vt.&vi.* 把……嵌入，栽种
embedded [ɪmˈbedɪd] *adj.* 植入的，深入的；内含的
fragment [ˈfrægmənt] *n.* 碎片；片段；未完成的部分
clause [klɔːz] *n.* 从句，分句；条款，款项
abandoned [əˈbændənd] *adj.* 被抛弃的；无约束的
acquisition [ˌækwɪˈzɪʃən] *n.* 获得物，获得
visible [ˈvɪzəbl] *adj.* 明显的，看得见的；现有的
multiple [ˈmʌltɪpl] *adj.* 多重的；多样的；许多的
rare [reə] *adj.* 罕见的，稀有的；半熟的
　　rare word 生僻词
assume [əˈsjuːm] *vt.* 承担；假定；采取；呈现
　　　　　　　vi. 装腔作势；多管闲事
proficiency [prəˈfɪʃənsɪ] *n.* 精通，熟练
neat [niːt] *adj.* 灵巧的；齐整的；整洁的；优雅的
neatly [ˈniːtlɪ] *adv.* 整洁地；干净地；灵巧地
reveal [rɪˈviːl] *vt.* 显示；透露；揭露；泄露

hierarchical [ˌhaɪəˈrɑːkɪkl] *adj.* 分层的；分等级的
receptive vocabulary 接受性词汇
relatively [ˈrelətɪvlɪ] *adv.* 相当地；相对地
mechanics of representation 表述的技巧（方法）
identify [aɪˈdentɪfaɪ] *vt.* 确定；识别；使参与
　　　　　　　　　　 vi. 确定；认同；一致
explicit [ɪkˈsplɪsɪt; ek-] *adj.* 明确的；清楚的
gnashing teeth 磨牙症
roar [rɔː] *n.* 咆哮；吼；轰鸣
　　　　　vi.& vt. 咆哮；吼叫；喧闹
issue [ˈɪʃuː] *n.* 问题；议题
be mapped to 被映射到……
nominalisation [ˌnɒmɪnəlaɪˈzeɪʃən] *n.* 名词化；名物化
lexical [ˈleksɪk(ə)l] *adj.* 词汇的；[语] 词典的
　　lexical item 词条，词项
lyrical [ˈlɪrɪkl] *adj.* 热情奔放的；感情丰富的
direct speech 直接引语
rumpus [ˈrʌmpəs] *n.* <口> 喧嚣，吵闹
convention [kənˈvenʃn] *n.* 国际公约；惯例
punctuation [ˌpʌŋktʃʊˈeɪʃn] *n.* 标点符号；标点法
bold [bəʊld] *adj.* 明显的，醒目的，勇敢的
　　　　　　 n. 粗体字；黑体字
font [fɒnt] *n.* 字体；字形

Ideological and Political Concept

　　语言是交流和思维的工具，也是文化的载体，幼儿语言能力的发展对其他领域的学习和发展产生重要的影响。教师应该在教学实践活动中有意识地融入我国优秀传统文化元素，树立文化自信心，培养正确的人生观和价值观。由于幼儿期是语言发展关键期，教师在弘扬民族文化的同时，可以让幼儿接触其他语言，了解世界的多元文化，为幼儿开启一扇了解世界的窗口。在教学实践中，教师应引导学生正确看待不同文化价值观之间的差异，从而培养幼儿的批判性思维。

Part 3　English Proficiency

Morphology

Word Building Ⅶ 构词（七）

Clipping 截短法

1. Definition 定义

> Clipping is to shorten a long word by cutting a part off the original and use what has remained as a word. These shortened words are called clippings. Sometimes a clipping drives out its longer original and becomes a standard word in its own right.
>
> 截短法就是去除原有单词的一部分，然后使剩下来的那部分代替原有单词。这些被截短的单词被称为截短词。有时截短词会取代相应较长的原始词，本身成为标准词。

2. Types of Clipping 截短法的分类

(1) front clippings 截头：This shortening may occur at the beginning of the word.

　　telephone → **phone** 电话　　　　　　ai**rplane** → **plane** 飞机

　　ear**thquake** → **quake** 地震

(2) back clippings 去尾：This shortening may occur at the end of the word.

　　mathematics → **maths** 数学　　　　**taxi**cab → **taxi** 出租车

　　examination → **exam** 检查；考试　　**ad**vertisement → **ad**. 广告

　　kilogram → **kilo** 千克（公斤）　　　**gent**lemen → **gent** 绅士；先生

　　laboratory → **lab** 实验室　　　　　**dorm**itory → **dorm** 宿舍

(3) front and back clippings 截头去尾：This shortening may occur at both ends of the word.

　　in**flu**enza → **flu** 流感　　　　　　re**frige**rator → **fridge** 冰箱

　　pre**script**ion → **script** 处方

(4) syncope 中间截短：This shortening may occur in the middle of the word.

　　pacificist → **pacifist** 和平主义者　　**spec**tacles → **specs** 眼镜

(5) phrase clippings 短语截短：A number of phrases have been made into one word.

　　public house → **pub** 酒吧　　　　　**pop**ular music → **pop** 流行音乐

(6) journalist clipping 新闻截短：Many journalist clippings can be seen in newspapers.

　　Department → **Dept** 部门　　　　　　Hong Kong → **H.K.** 香港

Non-finite Verb | 非谓语动词（一）

在句子中充当除谓语以外的各种句子成分的动词形式，叫做非谓语动词 (Non-finite Verb)。非谓语形式有四种：动词不定式、动名词、现在分词和过去分词。非谓语动词都是非限定动词，它们具有双重性。既有动词的一些特征，又具有名词、形容词、副词等的语法功能。非谓语动词与谓语动词是相对的概念。

Infinitive（Inf.）动词不定式
动词不定式没有词形变化。它之所以被称为不定式，是因为动词不被限定，或者说不被词形变化所局限。不定式属于非谓语动词。

1. 动词不定式的构成

以"do"为例	主动	被动	与谓语动作关系
一般式	(to) + do	(to) be done	同时发生，或之后发生
进行式	(to) be doing	/	同时发生
完成式	(to) have done	(to) have been done	之前发生
完成进行式	(to) have been doing	/	之前发生并持续或影响至今
否定式	not + (to) do	not + (to) be done	

一般式：
- We plan *to pay* a visit. 我们计划去参观。（主动）
- He wants *to be* an artist. 他想成为一个艺术家。（主动）
- The patient asked *to be operated* on at once. 病人要求马上手术。（被动）
- The teacher ordered the work *to be done*. 老师要求完成工作。（被动）

进行式：
- The boy pretended *to be working* hard. 男孩假装工作得很努力。（主动）
- He seems *to be reading* in his room. 看起来他正在他的房间里面读书。（主动）
- He was happy *to be coming* home. 就要回家了，他感到高兴。（主动）

完成式：
- I happened *to have seen* the film. 我偶然看过这部电影。（主动）
- He is pleased *to have met* his friend. 他很高兴能遇上他的朋友。（主动）
- The switch seemed *to have been thrown* in her. 那头假发似乎已经长在她的头上了。（被动）

完成进行式：
- He seems *to have been doing* nothing but reading. 他好像除了一直在读书之外什么都没做。（主动）
- The president was reported *to have been flying* across the Atlantic. 据报道，总统一直在飞越大西洋。（主动）
- The battle was said *to have been going* on for two days. 据说战斗已经进行两天了。（主动）

2. 动词不定式的语法功能

功能	特征	示例
作主语	真主语	*To lose* your heart means failure. / It means failure *to lose* your heart. 灰心意味着失败。 It took him four hours *to go* there and back. 他往返花了4个小时。 It's kind of you *to help* me move the box. 你真好心来帮我搬箱子。
作表语	表示情态	Her job is *to clean* the hall. 她的工作是打扫大厅。（内容） These books are *not to be sold*. 不应该卖掉这些书。（应该） Children are *not to smoke*. 儿童不准吸烟。（禁止） He appears *to have caught* a cold. 他似乎感冒了。（推测）
作宾语	动宾介宾有时省宾	She doesn't like *to be treated* as a child. 她不喜欢被当作孩子对待。 I have no choice but *to stay* here. 我只能留在这里，别无选择。 He did nothing yesterday but *repair* his bike. 他昨天除了修自行车什么也没干。 This should help *(to) reduce* the pain. 这个应有助于减轻疼痛。 He gave us some advice on *how to learn* English. 他给了我们学英语的建议。
做宾补	动宾介宾有时省宾	He won't allow himself *to fail*. 他不会任由自己失败的。 We invite you *to try* it out soon! 我们邀请您现在就开始试用！ With the work *to do*, he didn't go to the cinema. 他有工作要做，所以没去电影院。 I saw him *cross* the road. 我看见他横过公路。 He was seen *to cross* the road. 他被我看见横过公路。
作定语	后置	I have a meeting *to attend*. 我有一个会议要出席。 He found a good house *to live in*. 他找到了一个居住的好房子。 He has no money and no place *to live (in)*. 他没有钱，也没有地方住。 Have you got anything *to send*? 你要送什么东西吗？ Have you got anything *to be sent*? 你有什么东西需要送吗？
作状语	各种类型	He came *to help* me with maths. 他来帮我学习数学。（目的） He is old enough *to go* to school. 他到了上学的年龄。（结果） I visited him only *to find* him out. 我去拜访他，只见他出去了。（结果） They were very sad *to hear* the news. 他们听到这条新闻非常伤心。（原因） It's too dark for us *to see* anything. 太暗了，我们什么也看不见。（程度）
独立成分	立场态度	*To tell you the truth,* what I said at the meeting was not my opinion. 说实话，我在会上说的并不是我的意见。 *To make the matter worse,* he locked his keys in the car. 更糟糕的是，他把钥匙锁在车里了。

3. 常见不定式的省略用法

省略 do：If you don't want to do it, you don't need *to*. 如果你不想做这件事，你就不必做。

You needn't talk to anyone if you don't want *to*. 不想说话的时候，你可以不说。

省略 to：

并列使用时：He wished to study medicine and *become* a doctor. 他希望学医并成为医生。

To try and *fail* is better than not to try at all. 尝试而失败总比不尝试好。

使役动词后：Let's *go*！走吧！

They made him *tell* them everything. 他们强迫他把一切全告诉他们。

He was made *to work* twenty hours a day. 他被要求每天工作20个小时。(被动时不可省)

感官动词后：Did you notice her *leave* the house? 她离开屋子你注意到了吗？
　　　　　　I watched her *get* into the car. 我看着她上了车。
　　　　　　We all felt the house *shake*. 我们都感觉这房子在震动。
　　　　　　They all felt the plan *to be* unwise. 他们都认为这个计划不明智。
　　　　　　（to be 不可省）

why (not) 后：Why *let* such trifles worry you so much? 这点小事你怎么就急成那样儿了。
　　　　　　Why *not have* a try? 为什么不试一试？

except /but 后：I could do nothing except *agree*. 我除了同意，没有别的办法。（前是 do）
　　　　　　We can do nothing but *chance* it. 我们只有碰碰运气了。（前是 do）
　　　　　　I have no choice but *to sign* the contract. 我别无选择，只能签合同。
　　　　　　（前非 do 不可省）

help 后可省：Can you help *(to) carry* this table upstairs? 你能帮忙把桌子搬到楼上去吗？
　　　　　　She helped *(to) organize* the party. 她协助筹备了晚会。
　　　　　　The farmers were helped *to pick* apples. 农民们摘苹果时得到了帮助。
　　　　　　（被动时不可省）

4. 不定式复合结构

（1）当不定式动作不是句子主语发出时，需要加上自己的逻辑主语来构成不定式复合结构：
　　例如：
　　　　for + 名词（或代词宾格）+ 不定式
　　　　of + 名词（或代词宾格）+ 不定式

（2）不定式复合结构的语法功能如下：

主语：*For a child to learn everything* is impossible. 一个小孩要学会所有的东西是不可能的。
　　　It's impossible *for a child to learn everything*
　　　It was very cruel *of them to eat rare wild animals*. 他们吃稀有野生动物真够残忍的。
宾语：I don't think it advisable *for him to learn medicine*. 我认为他学医不合适。
表语：This is *for you to decide*. 这得由你决定。
状语：She waved the red flag *for the car to stop*. 她挥动红旗让车停下来。
　　　The article is too difficult *for me to understand*. 这篇文章太难，我理解不了。
定语：The order *for them to climb the mountain* was given. 让他们登山的命令已经发出。

5. 疑问词 + 不定式结构

疑问词后加不定式构成一种特殊的不定式短语，在句中用作主语、宾语和表语。

e.g. *When to start* has not been decided. 何时动身尚未决定。（主语）
　　　I don't know *what to do*. 我不知道该怎么办。（宾语）
　　　I can tell you *where to get this book*. 我可以告诉你哪里可以买到此书。（直接宾语）
　　　The difficulty was *how to cross the river*. 困难在于如何过河。（表语）

Gerund 动名词

动名词由动词变化而来，是非谓语动词的一种，具有双重性，既具有动词的某些特征，又具有名词的句法功能。

1. 动名词的构成

以"do"为例	主动	被动	与谓语动作关系
一般式	doing	being done	与谓语动作同时发生
完成式	having done	having been done	在谓语之前发生并持续或影响至今
否定式	not doing	not being done	

2. 动名词的动词特征

（1）可以带宾语：Learning *English* is difficult.

（2）可以被状语修饰：I have got used to living *in the countryside*. 我已经习惯住在乡村了。

（3）可以加逻辑主语构成复合结构：

Mary's being late again made her teacher very angry. 玛丽的再次迟到使她的老师非常生气。

Do you mind *my (me) opening* the door? 我开门，你介意吗？

（4）有时态和语态的变化：

Seeing is *believing*. 眼见为实。（一般式）

He came to the party without *being invited*. 他未被邀请就来到了晚会。（被动式）

We remembered *having seen* the film. 我们记得看过这部电影。（完成式）

He forgot *having been taken* to Guangzhou. 他忘记曾被带到广州去过。（完成被动式）

I regret *not following* his advice. 我后悔没听他的劝告。（否定式）

Not being seen by any one, he escaped. 他趁无人看见时逃跑了。（被动否定式）

3. 动名词的语法功能

功能	特征	示例
作主语	主语 真主语	*Reading* is an art. 读书是一种艺术。 *Climbing mountains* is really fun. 爬山真是有趣。 It is no use/no good *crying over spilt milk*. 覆水难收。 There is *no saying* when he'll come. 很难说他何时回来。 *Their coming to help* was a great encouragement to us. 他们来帮忙，对我们是极大的鼓舞。
作宾语	动词宾语	They ceased *talking /to talk*. 他们停止说话。 They went on walking and never stopped *talking*. 他们继续走，说个不停。 I found it pleasant *walking* along the seashore. 在海滩上走真是乐事。 to do：一次性/特指；doing：一般性/泛指/进行中
	介词宾语	The rain prevented us from *completing the work*. 下雨妨碍我们完成工作。 She complains of *the book being too difficult*. 她抱怨这本书太难。 On *leaving school*, he went into business. 一离开学校，他就投身商业中去了。
	固定搭配	The music is well *worth listening to* more than once. 这曲子很值得多听几遍。 We *are busy preparing* for the coming sports meet. 我们正为马上到来的运动会做着准备。

续表

功能	特征	示例
作表语	主/表一致对等	In the ant city, the queen's job is **laying eggs**. 在蚂蚁王国，蚁后的工作是产卵。 What I hate most is **being laughed at**. 我最痛恨的就是被别人嘲笑。 **Seeing** is **believing**。(**To see** is **to believe**.) 眼见为实。
作定语	表示某种用途	He can't walk without a **walking** stick. 他没有拐杖不能走路。 Is there a **swimming** pool in your school? 你们学校有游泳池吗？ a **walking** stick = a stick for **walking** = a stick which is used for **walking**

Part 4 Unit Practice

1. Read aloud and write down the following words according to the phonics.

   certain / turn / support / hare / source / sour / hour / clear / tire / wear

   [mɑ:kɪt] _____   [nə:s] _____   [ʃɔ:t] _____

   [keə] _____   [dɪə] _____   [auə] _____

2. Put the school languages into English.

   你喜欢什么颜色？   请把剪刀递给我。
   我要画一个苹果。   把你的名字写在画上。
   把纸对折再打开。   请把铅笔放回去。

3. Put the following phrases and sentences into Chinese.

   （1）the importance of phonological awareness

   （2）There is a difference between oral and written language syntax.

   （3）In oral language, meanings can be expressed through gestures, facial expressions and intonations.

   （4）Written language provides models of syntax and vocabulary which then become used in oral language.

4. Read the clipping words and name them.

   gas _____   bus _____   lunch _____

   memo _____   cab _____   Dept _____

   gent _____   ad _____   kilo _____

5. Rewrite the sentences according to the tips in the bracket.

   （1）It was very strange that she should have said that. (using the infinitive)

   　　It was very strange _____ that.

   （2）The idea is that we should meet on Thursday. (using the infinitive)

   　　The idea is _____ on Thursday.

   （3）I'm surprised to find it easy that they will work on it in a short time. (using the infinitive)

   　　I'm surprised to find it easy _____ on it in a short time.

   （4）The girl opened the door so that the little cat could go out. (using the infinitive)

   　　The girl opened the door _____.

(5) It was a pleasure that I had been invited to my best friend's wedding. (using the infinitive)
   It was a pleasure _____ to my best friend's wedding.

(6) That Jack didn't get to the station on time made all of us worried. (using the gerund)
   _____ the station on time made all of us worried.

(7) My worry is that you rely too much on your parents. (using the gerund)
   My worry is _____ too much on your parents.

(8) Would you mind if I opened the window for a little while? (using the gerund)
   Would you mind _____ the window for a little while?

Part 5 Extended Reading

Literacy Center

Through the Literacy Center children practice essential skills for reading, writing and spelling. They have the opportunity to reinforce and extend these skills while working independently or in small groups. The Literacy Center activities enable children to confidently move toward becoming successful readers and communicators.

Child Development

The Literacy Center offers many experiences to facilitate growth and enhance skills in all areas of development.

Physical Skills: strengthen eye-hand coordination, fine motor skills, visual discrimination and auditory discrimination.

Social/Emotional Skills: develop cooperation, self-control, self-esteem and confidence.

Language Skills: develop an understanding of the importance of sounds and print in communication, build vocabulary, sound memory, comprehension, listening skills and verbal expression.

Intellectual Skills: provide opportunities for naming, identifying, recalling, predicting, sequencing, patterning, decision making and creativity.

Points to Remember

- Clearly define the literacy center area.
- Change activities to maintain and stimulate interest.
- Provide multi-level activities to accommodate children's abilities.
- Introduce one item at a time, explaining and modeling the care and handling of the equipment and supplies.
- Provide a system for student accountability.

UNIT 7

- Children engage longer in activities that are meaningful, such as creating a menu, collecting phone numbers, or writing an original story.

Suggested Literacy Center Materials

- Books of all sizes and types
- Magazines and newspapers
- Pocket charts
- Sentence strips
- Pictures, words, and objects for sorting
- Letter tiles, stamps and stamp pads
- Writing materials
- Flannel board with pictures, letters and words
- Reading-the-Room pointers and "glasses"
- Tape recorder and blank tapes
- Tape players
- Commercial, teacher-created, and student-created tapes
- Phonics phone
- Wall charts (includes names, alphabet, environmental words, nursery rhymes, and poetry)
- Magnetic letters and boards
- Author's chair
- Eight-page mini books
- Sight-word list
- Picture dictionary
- Wallpaper samples
- Simple word searches
- Hole punch
- Class list of names
- Graphs
- Grids
- Venn-Diagrams
- Story maps
- Flip books
- Placemats
- Popsicle sticks
- Diary
- Games
- Overhead projector
- Greeting cards
- Sliding masks or flags
- Story prompts
- Sign language chart
- Modeling clay
- Letter and number cutters
- Computer
- Paper money and coins
- School staff poster with names
- Sand trays
- Salt trays
- Blank books for student-made books
- Paper
- Crayons, markers, pens, pencils
- Interesting or unusual writing utensils
- Maps
- Magnifying glasses
- Labels
- Envelopes
- Recipes
- Menus
- Mailboxes
- Nameplates
- Notebooks
- Typewriters
- Journals
- Stapler
- Sticky notes
- Yarn
- Shoelaces
- Clipboards—full size and miniature
- Flyswatters with hole cut on die-cut machine for a pointer or sliding mask
- White boards and markers
- Pipe cleaners

135

UNIT 8

Teacher Handbook

> "Childhood is the most important of all life's seasons."
>
> —Unknown

Learning Objectives

Students will
- ★ review English phonemes
- ★ be familiar with school languages, chants, songs and stories
- ★ learn how to play a game for children
- ★ master new words and expressions
- ★ understand what the assessment of student competencies is and learn how to develop children's early writing skills
- ★ review word building and participles

Part 1   Skills for Pre-school English Teaching

Phonetics

English Phonics Ⅶ 自然拼读法（七）

Consonant Digraphs & Letter Teams 辅音字母及多字母组合的读音

Phonics		Examples	Phonics		Examples
ch	[tʃ]	China check teacher	cea	[ʃə]	ocean
ck	[k]	black clock cock pack	cia		facial official special
dge	[dʒ]	bridge judge knowledge	cient	[ʃənt]	ancient efficient sufficient
gn	[n]	Campaign foreign sign	gh	[g]	ghastly ghost ghee
ng	[ŋ(g)]	angry English ring thing long strong lung hungry		[f]	laugh cough rough
				silent	eight high though
kn	[n]	knee knife knock know	augh ough	[ɔː]	caught daughter taught brought ought thought
nk	[ŋk]	thank pink donkey drunk			
ph	[f]	elephant photo physics	gue	[g]	colleague vague vogue
qu	[kw]	equal queen require	que	[k]	antique technique unique
sion	[ʒən]	confusion conclusion vision decision revision television	ssion	[ʃən]	expression discussion impression profession
sh	[ʃ]	wash sheep dish shop	tch	[tʃ]	watch catch kitchen
th	[θ]	three thin thief mouth	tion	[ʃən]	action position station information situation
	[ð]	than the this brother			
wh	[w]	what wheel white who	ture	[tʃə]	future nature picture

School Languages

Snacks & Lunch 点心和午餐时间

- It's time to have a snack. /It time for lunch.
  该吃点心了。/ 午餐时间到了。
- Please wash your hands before you eat.
  吃东西前请洗手。
- Did you wash your hands?
  洗过手了吗?
- Remember to turn off the tap after washing.
  洗手后请记得关水龙头。
- Please drink some water.
  喝点水吧。
- Let's sing a song before we have snacks.
  吃点心前我们先来唱歌吧。
- Don't eat too much cookies. /Have some fruit.
  别吃太多饼干。/ 吃点水果吧。
- Fruit or cookies, which do you prefer?
  水果和饼干要哪个?
- Lunch is ready. Set the table. /Sit at the table.
  午餐准备好了。摆好桌子。/ 到桌子那里坐好。

- No talking while eating. You may choke on your food.
  吃饭时不要讲话，会呛到食物。
- What would you like to eat?
  你想吃什么?
- Do you want more rice?
  你要再吃点米饭吗?
- It's good for your health.
  吃这个对你的身体好。
- Take your time. Enjoy your meal.
  不急，慢慢吃。
- Clean up what you drop after eating.
  吃完后把掉到桌子上的东西清理干净。

WHO STOLE THE COOKIES

Chants & Songs

Who Stole the Cookies 谁偷了罐子里的饼干

Who stole the cookies from the cookie jar?
Cindy stole the cookies from the cookie jar.
Who me? Yes, you. Not me. Then who?
Lindy stole the cookies from the cookie jar.
Who me? Yes, you. Not me. Then who?
Sally stole the cookies from the cookie jar.
Who me? Yes, you. Not me. Then who?

If You're Happy

1. If you're hap-py and you know it clap your hands   If you're
2. If you're hap-py and you know it stamp your feet   If you're
3. If you're hap-py and you know it nod your head   If you're
4. If you're hap-py and you know it say good bye   If you're

hap-py and you know it clap your hands   If you're hap-py and you know it and you
hap-py and you know it stamp your feet   If you're hap-py and you know it and you
hap-py and you know it nod your head   If you're hap-py and you know it and you
hap-py and you know it say good bye   If you're hap-py and you know it and you

real-ly wan-na show it, if you're hap-py and you know it clap your hands
real-ly wan-na show it, if you're hap-py and you know it stamp your feet
real-ly wan-na show it, if you're hap-py and you know it nod your head
real-ly wan-na show it, if you're hap-py and you know it say good bye

Mary Had A Little Lamb

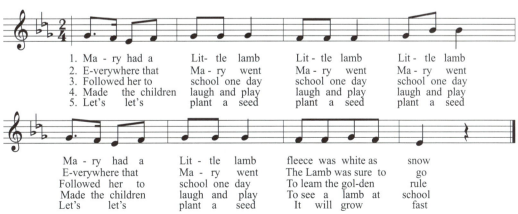

1. Ma-ry had a   Lit-tle lamb   Lit-tle lamb   Lit-tle lamb
2. E-verywhere that   Ma-ry went   Ma-ry went   Ma-ry went
3. Followed her to   school one day   school one day   school one day
4. Made the children   laugh and play   laugh and play   laugh and play
5. Let's let's   plant a seed   plant a seed   plant a seed

Ma-ry had a   Lit-tle lamb   fleece was white as   snow
E-verywhere that   Ma-ry went   The Lamb was sure to   go
Followed her to   school one day   To learn the gol-den   rule
Made the children   laugh and play   To see a lamb at   school
Let's let's   plant a seed   It will grow   fast

Stories

She Does Many Things After School
她放学后做很多事

She is busy after school. She comes home after school. She does her homework. She takes the dog for a walk. She feeds the dog. She eats dinner. She clears the table. She brushes her teeth. She watches TV. She watches for two hours only. Her parents allow her only two hours. She goes to bed.

I Want to Be Strong 我要变强壮

Tom's family was sitting together during dinnertime. Tom wasn't eating well. His mother said, "Tom, if you don't eat rice and vegetables, you won't grow to be big and strong!" "No! I hate eating... especially vegetables. Yuck!" Tom yelled back. It was 9 o'clock and Tom was ready for bed. As his mom tucked him in, she said, "Promise me you will eat better tomorrow. That's the only way you'll be strong and healthy!" "But... Mom... I don't want to eat rice." Tom mumbled as he fell asleep. Tom had a dream he was fighting a monster that took his puppy. He yelled and tried to get his puppy back, but it was useless. Tom was too weak and the monster laughed when Tom tried to fight him. "Ha ha," the monster laughed, "... children who don't eat their rice and vegetables can never defeat me!" The monster disappeared with Tom's puppy and Tom began to sob with sadness. At breakfast the next morning, Tom was eating well. "Wow, Tom, you are eating so well. I'm so proud of you!" "From now on, I'm going to eat everything on my plate because I want to grow up to be strong!" said Tom happily.

 Game

Simon Says 西蒙说

Objective: listening to the password and act

Rules: 1. Children stand in a line.

2. Appoint a child to be Simon who stands at the finish line to say the password "Simon says... (action instruction) ".

3. Children act as the password but only when they hear "Simon says". E.g: When they hear "Simon says 'take one step' (here can be any other action) " children quickly take one step toward the finish line. But if without "Simon says", children are not supposed to act, otherwise they must get back to the original point.

4. The first child to reach the finish line wins.

Language: Do as Simon says. /Do what you're told but only when Simon says!

Tips: The winner can be the leader of next round.

Instructions: Please watch the way my lips move carefully. I will just mouth a word /sentence without sound. As long as you guess it, shout it out loud as quickly as you can. If that's it, you'll get a Good Job Sticker. Furthermore, once you're the fastest, you'll win the first prize.

Part 2 Pre-school Education in English

Assessment of Student Competencies

Stages of Writing Development

The development of early writing skills is another aspect of your child's emergent literacy development. The following stages represent writing development in children. All stages overlap and children progress and reach writing stages at many different ages. Regardless of which stage your child is at, writing development can be enhanced through being encouraged to write on a regular basis. Children should never be discouraged from exploring writing by the means they are able to do, whether it be scribbling, letter strings, invented spelling, or conventional spelling.

Stage	Example
Preliterate: Drawing § uses drawing as a means of communicating § believes that drawings and writing is communication of a purposeful message § reads their drawings as if there were writing on them	
Preliterate: Scribbling § scribbles but intends it as writing § resembles writing § holds and uses a pencil like an adult	
Early Emergent: Letter-like forms § shapes in writing actually resemble letters § shapes are not actually letters § look like poorly formed letters, but are unique creations	
Emergent: **Random letters or letter strings** § uses letter sequences perhaps learned from his/her name § may write the same letter in many ways § long strings of letters in random order	
Transitional: **Invented spelling** § creates own spelling when conventional spelling is not known § one letter may represent an entire syllable § words may overlay § may not use proper spacing § as writing matures, more words are spelled conventionally § as writing matures, perhaps only one or two letters invented or omitted.	
Fluency: **Conventional spelling** § usually resembles adult writing	

Phonological Awareness

Speaking and listening skills provide the foundation for literacy. Studies have shown that reading outcomes for children can be predicted by their early language ability. Some children may need to be specifically taught phonological awareness skills. Phonological awareness is an awareness of sound and an awareness that words:

- can be broken up into syllables, (hos-pit-al)
- can rhyme, (can, fan, man)
- can start with the same sound, (never, naughty)
- can be broken up into first sound or sounds and the rhyme pattern

  e.g. (s-and) (st-and)

- can be formed by blending separate sounds together

e.g. (f-i-s-h or f-ish makes fish)

• can be segmented into separate sounds (s-a-n-d)

• can be changed around by adding, removing or re-ordering sounds to make new words

e.g. (minus s, sand = and, change a to e sand = send)

Activities to Develop Phonological Awareness

Read the story:

• *Each, Peach, Pear, Plum*, Janet & Alan Ahlberg

• *Goodness Gracious*, Phil Cummings

• *Where's my Teddy*? Jez Alborough

• *Don't forget the Bacon*, Pat Hutchins

• *Pass the Jam Jim*, Kaye Umansky & Margaret Chamberlain

• *Animalia*, Graeme Base

• *Can You Hear Me Grandad*? Pat Thompson.

After children become familiar with the story, encourage them to provide the rhyming words at the end of each sentence, e.g. "Hairy Mclairy from Donaldson's... " and "Hercules Morse as big as a... "

Play games and activities:

• clapping and playing instruments to names: el-e-phant, Is-a-bell-a

• children grouping by the number of syllables in their name as part of daily routines

　　e.g. "Get your lunch if you have 3 parts to your name."

• making up rhymes, e.g. man, fan, pan, Dan.

• matching items/pictures by rhyme, e.g. house/mouse, dog/log.

• making up sentences with children's names using alliterations, e.g. Sally slides slowly, Joshua jumps, Billy bounces.

• Sound Bucket Game. Pull out an object, name it and find its starting sound. Think of another word that begins with the same sound. Are there any other things in the bucket that begin with the same sound?

• Sound Basket or table. All items on the table or in the basket need to start with the same letter.

• The Letter Shop. Chose a letter and then see how many things might be sold at the shop that start with that letter, e.g. the L shop has lollies, lettuce, licorice, lasagna, lemons.

Pencil Grip Stages

Latest research says any grip is acceptable as long as it is functional and stable, i.e. the pencil does not slip; the child has control and can write without tiring.

1. Palmer Grasp

Stage one

Pencil is held across the palm, holding the top end. The tip of the pencil is pointing down, with the thumb facing upwards.

Stage two

Pencil is held with the thumb on one side and all the other fingers on the other side. The palm faces down.

2. Tripod Grip

Stage one

As the child grows and develops, there is a gradual progression from grasping to gripping. The thumb opposes the index finger with the pencil held between them. The middle finger may extend down the shaft or support the pencil along the side of the finger.

Generally, there is more control towards the tip of the pencil. Whole arm movements are still used, with little control over the small muscles of the hand.

Stage two

Once again, the progression is a gradual one. In stage two of the grip, less whole arm movements occur because the shoulder, elbow and then the wrist become more stable to provide a fixed posture.

3. Mature Grip

The thumb opposes the index to hold the pencil resting on the middle finger. There are refined small movements of the thumb and index finger for control. The fourth and fifth fingers reinforce the middle finger.

Notes

1. Background

The Early Years Learning Framework for Australia (EYLF) is a pedagogical framework for curriculum planning and programming and underpins the child centred play-based program. The EYLF must be used by all Transition and Pre-school teachers. This Handbook provides comprehensive information on each of the assessment criteria along with recommended classroom activities, assessment suggestions and recommended resources. The teaching activities provide ways in which students can practise and be observed (assessed) against each of the competencies. Individual and class-based intervention actions for each indicator are included in the Handbook.

澳大利亚的早期学习框架(EYLF)是课程规划和课程设计的一个教学框架，是以儿童为中心的以游戏为基础的课程。所有的过渡和学前教师都必须使用EYLF。这本手册提供了关于每一个评估标准的综合信息，以及推荐的课堂活动、评估建议和推荐的资源。教学活动提供了学生可以练习并且用来进行观察（评估）的针对每一项能力的方法。手册中包括了针对个体及基于班级的每项指标的干预措施。

2. *Regardless of* which stage your child is at, writing development can be enhanced through being encouraged to write on a regular basis.

不管你的孩子处于哪个阶段，通过鼓励定期写作都可以加强写作的发展。

  regardless of 不管，不顾；无；不拘

  e.g. Regardless of whether he is right or wrong, we have to abide by his decisions.

  不管他正确与否，我们都得服从他的决定。

3. Children should never be discouraged from exploring writing *by the means* they are able to do, whether it be scribbling, letter strings, invented spelling, or conventional spelling.

儿童永远不应该被阻止用他们能够做的方式来探索写作，无论是涂鸦、字母串、自创的拼写，还是常规的拼写。

  by the means... / by means of... 以……方式，通过……手段

e.g. We express our thoughts by means of words. 我们用词句来表达思想。

by all means = certainly

e.g. Go ahead by all means. 你只管干下去。

by no means = not ... at all

e.g. I am by no means an unsociable person. 我绝对不是一个不合群的人。

4. ... reads their drawings as if there were writing on them.

阅读他们的图画，就好像他们在写东西一样。

as if 从句用作虚拟语气。 当说话人认为句子所述的是不真实的或极少有可能发生或存在的情况时，如果从句表示与现在事实相反，谓语动词用一般过去时。

如：You look as if you didn't care. 你看上去好像并不在乎。

He talks as if he knew where she was. 他说话的样子，好像他知道她在哪里似的。

5. Latest research says any grip is acceptable as long as it is functional and stable, i.e. the pencil does not slip, the child has control and can write without tiring.

最新的研究表明，只要能使用并且能握稳，任何握笔方式都是可以接受的，即铅笔不滑落；孩子能控制；写字不累。

as long as / so long as 引导条件状语从句，意为"只要"。

e.g. You can take my car as /so long as you drive carefully.

你可以用我的汽车，只要你小心点儿开。

Useful Words & Expressions

assessment [əˈsesmənt] *n*. 评估；评价

emergent literacy 早期读写能力

stage [steɪdʒ] *n*. 阶段；舞台；戏剧

overlap [ˌəʊvəˈlæp] *n*. 重叠部分；覆盖物
     vi. & *vt*. 重叠；与……部分相同

enhance [ɪnˈhɑːns] *vt*. 提高；加强

discourage [dɪsˈkʌrɪdʒ] *vt*. 阻止；使气馁

scribble [ˈskrɪb(ə)l] *n*. 潦草写成的东西
     vi. & *vt*. 乱写；乱涂；潦草书写

conventional [kənˈvenʃnl] *adj*. 传统的；习用的，
       平常的；约定的

preliterate [priːˈlɪtərət] *adj*. 文字出现以前的

purposeful [ˈpɜːpəsfl] *adj*. 有目的的，故意的
     adv. 果断地，有明确目标地

intend [ɪnˈtend] *vt*. 打算；想要；意指

resemble [rɪˈzembl] *vt*. 与……相像，类似于

letter-like 类似字母的，像字母的

poorly formed 形式不佳的，形式不正确的

unique creation 独特的创作

random [ˈrændəm] *adj*. 随机的；任意的；胡乱的

sequence [ˈsiːkwəns] *n*. 顺序；序列；连续

transitional [trænˈzɪʃənl] *adj*. 变迁的；过渡期的

syllable [ˈsɪləbl] *n*. 音节

mature [məˈtʃʊə] *adj*. 成熟的；成年人的
     vi. 成熟；到期
     vt. 使……成熟；使……长成

omit [ə(ʊ)ˈmɪt] *vt*. 省略；遗漏；删除；疏忽

fluency [ˈfluːənsɪ] *n*. 流畅，流利

outcome [ˈaʊtkʌm] *n*. 结果，结局；成果

predict [prɪˈdɪkt] *vt.* & *vi*. 预言；预示，预告

specifically [spəˈsɪfɪklɪ] *adv*. 特有地，明确地

rhyme [raɪm] *n*. 韵脚；韵文；押韵词

v. 押韵；作押韵诗
blend [blend] *vt.* 混合；（使）调和；协调
　　　　　　　vi. 掺杂；结合；相配，相称
　　　　　　　n. 混合；混合物；混合色
segment [ˈsegmənt] *n.* 环节；部分，段落
　　　　　　　vt.&vi. 分割，划分
minus [ˈmaɪnəs] *prep.* （表示否定）没有；缺少；
　　　　　　　（表示运算）减去；
　　　　　　　（表示数目）零度以下
　　　　　　　n. 减号；负号；不利；不足
　　　　　　　adj. 负的，不利的；不达标的
alliteration [əˌlɪtəˈreɪʃn] *n.* 头韵

bucket [ˈbʌkɪt] *n.* 水桶；一桶（的量）
i.e. (that is) *adv.* 也就是；abbr. (拉丁)
grip [grɪp] *n.* 握力；紧握，抓牢；掌握
　　　　　　　vi.&vt. 握紧，抓牢；吸引住
Palmer [ˈpɑːmə] *n.* 人名；帕尔默
grasp [grɑːsp] *vt.* 抓住
　　　　　　　n. 控制；控制力；能力所及
　　　　　　　vi. 攫取（常与 at 连用）
tripod [ˈtraɪpɒd] *n.* [摄] 三脚架；三脚凳
oppose [əˈpəʊz] *vt.&vi.* 抵制；反对；使相对
shaft [ʃɑːft] *n.* 柄，轴；矛，箭

Ideological and Political Concept

教师应增强对语言领域教育目标指导性的认识和重视，并在教育教学实践中不偏离总目标的指导。幼儿语言能力的发展既要重视培养语言基础知识和基本技能，也要注重优化学习过程，引导幼儿形成有效的学习策略和一定的文化意识，培养积极向上的情感态度和正确的价值观。

Part 3　English Proficiency

Word Building Ⅷ 构词（八）

Acronymy—首字母缩略法

Acronymy is the process of forming new words by joining the initial letters of phrases.
用词组首字母组成新词的英语构词法叫做首字母缩略法。

Types of Acronymy 首字母缩略法的分类

(1) Initialisms: Initialisms are words pronounced letter by letter. 每个首字母分别发音的缩略词。

WHO [ˈdʌblju: eitʃ əʊ] ← **W**orld **H**ealth **O**rganization 世界卫生组织
GRE [ˌdʒi: ɑːrˈiː] ← **G**raduate **R**ecord **E**xamination 美国研究生入学考试
PDF [ˌpi: di: ˈef] ← **P**robability **D**istribution **F**unction 可移植文档格式文件
RPM [ˈɑːrˈpi: ˈem] ← **R**evolutions **P**er **M**inute 每分钟转数

GDP [ˌdʒiː diːˈpiː] ← **G**ross **D**omestic **P**roduct 国内生产总值

(2) Acronyms: Acronyms are words formed from initial letters but pronounced as a normal word. 可以作为一个单词拼读发音的缩略词。

TOEFL [ˈtəʊfl] ← **T**esting of **E**nglish as a **F**oreign **L**anguage 托福考试
（美国检定非英语为母语者的英语能力考试）

TEFL [ˈtefl] ← **T**eaching **E**nglish as a **F**oreign **L**anguage 国际认可的通用英语教师资格考试之一

TESL [ˈtesl] ← **T**eaching **E**nglish as a **S**econd **L**anguage 作为第二语言的英语教学

BRICS [bˈrɪks] (**B**razil, **R**ussia, **I**ndia, **C**hina and **S**outh **A**frica) 金砖五国

Non-finite Verb Ⅱ 非谓语动词（二）

Present Participle (ppr.) 现在分词

现在分词由动词变化而来，是非谓语动词的一种，具有双重性，既具有动词的某些特征，又具有形容词和副词的句法功能。

以 "do" 为例	主动	被动	与谓语动作关系
一般式	doing	being done	与谓语动作同时发生
完成式	having done	having been done	在谓语之前发生并持续或影响至今
否定式	not doing	not being done	

e.g. They went to the park, *singing and talking*. 他们边唱边说向公园走去。（一般）

Having done his homework, he played basketball. 做完作业，他开始打篮球。（完成）

The problem *being discussed* is very important. 正在被讨论的问题很重要。（被动）

He also took exception to *having been spied on*. 他也讨厌被暗中监视。（完成被动）

Forgive me *for not seeing him off*. 原谅我没为他送行。（一般否定）

Not having done it right, I tried again. 我由于没有做对，所以又试了试。（完成否定）

The thief escaped, *not being seen* by anyone. 那个贼趁无人看见时逃跑了。（被动否定）

1. 现在分词的动词特征

(1) 可以带宾语：She sat there *reading a novel*. 她坐在那儿看小说。

(2) 可以被状语修饰：I'll paint what I have seen here, of course, the things *impressing me most*.
我要画我在这里所见到的，当然是我印象最深的。

(3) 可以加逻辑主语：*Jane's being so careless* caused so much trouble.
简的粗心造成了这么多的麻烦。

(4) 有时态和语态变化：*Having been told* many times, he still did not know how to do it.
已经告诉他多少次了，他还是不知道怎么做。

2. 现在分词（ppr.）与动名词（ger.）的对比

现在分词与动名词的构成方式相同，即"动词+ing（V.-ing）"；二者都保留着动词的一些特征，

在句中都能作定语和表语。

（1）定语：现在分词说明被修饰名词的动作；而动名词说明被修饰名词的性质和用途等。

e.g. a moving blackboard = a blackboard which is moving 移动的黑板（ppr.）

a swimming pool = a pool for swimming 游泳池（ger.）

（2）表语：动名词作表语说明主语的内容，回答 what 的问题，表语和主语几乎处于同等地位，可以互换位置，其句意不变；现在分词作表语相当于形容词作表语，说明主语的性质、特征等，回答 how 的问题，表语和主语不能互换位置。

e.g. My job is teaching. = Teaching is my job. 我的工作是教书。（ger.）

The play is exciting. ≠ (Exciting is the play.) 这部戏激动人心。（ppr.）

3. 现在分词的语法功能

功能	特征	示例
作定语	短语后置	In the *following* years he worked even harder. 在后来的几年中，他学习更努力了。 The man *speaking to the teacher* is our monitor's father. 正与老师谈话的那个人是我们班长的父亲。 the man *speaking to the teacher* = the man *who is speaking to the teacher*
作表语	性质状态	The argument is very *convincing*. 他的论点很令人信服。 The results have been *encouraging*. 结果令人振奋。 The film is *moving*. 这电影很感人。（表语，说明主语的性质） They are *moving* next Sunday. 他们下个周日搬家。（谓语，表示动作）
补足语	主补宾补	He was found *trying to* escape. 他试图逃走时被发现。（主补） With winter *coming* on, it's time to buy warm clothes.（介词 with 的宾补） 随着冬天的到来，是时候买暖和的衣服了。 I saw her *crossing* the road. 我看见她在过马路。（宾补） I saw her *cross* the road. 我看见她过了马路。（不定式作宾补）
作状语	主语一致	*Walking in the street*, I saw him. 当我在街上走时，我看到他了。（时间） *Being ill*, she stayed at home.（因为）生病，她留在家里。（原因） *Having failed many times*, he didn't lost heart. 有很多次失败，他没有灰心。（让步） His friend died, *getting him a lot of money*. 他的朋友死了，给了他很多钱。（结果） *Working hard*, you will succeed.（只要）努力工作，你就会成功。（条件） Please answer the question *using another way*. 请用另一种方式回答这个问题。（方式） Look at the people *lying on the beach*. 看那些人正躺在沙滩上。（伴随） He went *swimming the other day*. 几天前他去游泳了。（目的）
独立成分	语气情绪	*Judging from (by) his appearance*, he must be an actor. 从外表看，他一定是个演员。 *Generally speaking*, girls are more careful. 一般说来，女孩子更细心。 *Considering what you get*, this is quite a bargain. 考虑你能得到的，这是一笔好买卖。

Past Participle (pp.) 过去分词

过去分词是分词的一种。规则动词的过去分词一般是"动词+ed"构成，不规则动词的变化各有不同。过去分词是非谓语动词，有被动和完成的语义，具有形容词和副词的语法功能。

1. 过去分词的构成

(1) 规则变化。

结尾	变化规则	示例
一般动词	-ed	work → worked
不发音 "e"	-d	live → lived
辅音字母 + y	y → i-ed	cry → cried
重读闭音节 单辅音字母 非 r、y、x	双辅音字母 +ed	stop → stopped drop → dropped
c	c → ck-ed	picnic → picnicked traffic → trafficked

(2) 不规则变化（原形、过去式、过去分词）。

AAA	ABB	ABC	AAB
hit hit hit	sit sat sat	do did done	
let let let	feel felt felt	fall fell fallen	beat beat beaten
set set set	have had had	fly flew flown	
put put put	hold held held	take took taken	ABA
cost cost cost	burn burnt burnt	get got gotten	
hurt hurt hurt	hear heard heard	be was/were been	come came come
shut shut shut	find found found	drink drank drunk	become became become
read read read	make made made	begin began begun	
[red] [red]	catch caught caught	speak spoke spoken	

2. 过去分词的语法功能

功能	特征	示例
表语	状态	They were *frightened* at the sad sight. 他们对眼前悲惨的景象感到害怕。 The window is *broken*. 窗户破了。（状态） [The window was *broken* by the boy.（动作）]
作定语	分词后置短语	We must adapt our thinking to the *changed* conditions. 我们必须使我们的思想适应变化了的情况。 The concert *given* by their friends was a success. 他们朋友举行的音乐会大为成功。 The boy looked up with a *satisfied* expression. 男孩带着满意的表情举目而视。

续表

功能	特征	示例
状语	主语一致	***Written*** in a hurry, this article was not so good! 因为写得匆忙，这篇文章不是很好。（原因） ***Given*** another hour, I can also work out this problem. 再给我一个小时，我也能解开这道题。（条件） ***Seen*** from the top of the hill, the city looks more beautiful. 从山顶看城市，城市显得更漂亮。（方式） The signal ***given***, the bus started. 信号一发出，汽车就开动了。（时间） Her head ***held*** high, she went by. 她把头昂得高高地从这儿走了过去。（伴随） Though ***told*** of the danger, he still risked his life to save the boy. 虽然被告之有危险，他仍然冒生命危险去救那个孩子。（让步）
宾语补足语	介词宾补 动词宾补	I heard the song ***sung*** in English. 我听到有人用英语唱过这首歌。（感官） I'll have my hair ***cut*** tomorrow. 明天我要理发。（使役） I consider the matter ***settled***. 我认为这件事解决了。（主观） He didn't wish it ***mentioned***. 他不愿这事被提起。（意愿） He had his money ***stolen***. 他的钱被偷了。（被动） With the matter ***settled***, we all went home. 事情得到解决，我们都回家了。（原因）

3. 分词的独立主格结构

（1）独立主格结构含义：独立主格即独立结构（absolute construction），在句法上跟主句没有任何关系；但在意义上却与主句紧密相连，共同构成一个完整的语义环境。独立主格结构没有句法上的主语和谓语，只有逻辑上的主谓和动宾关系。因此，独立主格不是句子，而是一个独特结构形式。在句子中分词的逻辑主语不是句子的主语时，须使用独立主格结构。独立主格结构可置于句首、句尾，常用逗号与主句隔开。

（2）分词独立主格结构的形式。

a. 名词／代词＋现在分词：逻辑上是主谓关系。

Winter coming, it gets colder and colder. 冬天来了，天气越来越冷了。

The rain having stopped, he went out for a walk. 雨停了，他出去散步。

b. 名词／代词＋过去分词：逻辑上是动宾关系。

More time given, we should have done it much better.

如果给我们更多的时间，我们会做得更好。

The boy stood there, his right hand raised. 那个男孩站在那里，右手高举。

（3）独立主格结构的语法功能：独立主格结构相当于一个状语从句，在句子中做状语。

时间：***The question being settled***, we went home. 问题解决之后，我们就回家了。

Her work done, she sat down for a cup of tea. 她干完了活，坐下来喝茶。

条件：***Time permitting***, we'll do another two exercises. 如果时间允许，我们将做另两个练习。

More money given, we should have sent more employees to the mother company to get trained.

如果给我们更多的钱，我们就应该派更多的员工到母公司去接受培训。

原因：***Nobody having anymore to say***, the meeting closed. 因为再无人发言，会议结束。

The manager looks relaxed, ***many things settled***.

许多事情已经处理好了，经理看上去很轻松。

伴随：She ran up to me, ***her hair flying in the wind***. 她向我跑来，秀发在风中飘扬着。

He lay there, ***his teeth set, his hands clenched, his eyes looking straight up***.

他躺在那儿，牙关紧闭，双拳紧握，两眼直视上方。

Part 4 Unit Practice

1. Read aloud and write down the following words according to the phonics.

bridge / strong / knife / official / picture / laugh / these / peach / bath / sheet

[mauθ] _____   [ðɪs] _____   [wi:l] _____

[pæk] _____   [kætʃ] _____   [ʃi:p] _____

2. Put the school languages into English.

吃饭前请洗手。   汤别洒了。

洗手后记得关水龙头。   多吃点水果。

再喝点水吧。   别急，慢慢享用。

3. Put the following phrases and sentences into Chinese.

(1) child's emergent literacy development

(2) use drawing as a means of communicating

(3) phonological awareness skill

(4) Words can be broken up into syllables.

(5) Speaking and listening skills provide the foundation for literacy.

4. Read the acronyms and name them.

TOEFL _____   CD _____   VIP _____

AIDS _____   DVD _____   IQ _____

GDP _____   IT _____   EQ _____

5. Choose the best answer to complete the sentences.

(1) The weather _____ so bad, we had to put the game off.

  A. was   B. is   C. were   D. being

(2) There _____ no classes yesterday, we paid a visit to the Great Wall.

  A. was   B. being   C. were   D. had been

(3) The problem _____, the meeting came to the end.

  A. settled   B. was settled   C. being settled   D. setting

(4) The boy lay on the ground, his eyes _____ and his hands _____.

  A. being closed; trembling   B. closed; trembling

  C. closed; trembled   D. closing; trembled

(5) The country has already sent up three unmanned spacecraft, the most recent _____ at the end of last March.

   A. has been launched
   B. having been launched
   C. being launched
   D. to be launched

(6) _____, the work can be done much better.

   A. Given more time
   B. We had been given more time
   C. More time given
   D. If more time had given

(7) _____, he went and watched the game.

   A. His homework done
   B. Done his homework
   C. His homework doing
   D. If he will do his homework

(8) _____, she went to the cinema house.

   A. She finished her supper
   B. Finished supper
   C. Her supper finished
   D. To be finished her supper

Part 5　Extended Reading

Writing Center

Children love to write and read their writings to anyone who will listen. The Writing Center gives children the opportunity to communicate through writing in a variety of different experiences. The Writing Center encourages children's early interest in writing and provides a foundation that reinforces their beginning efforts and desire to write.

Child Development

The Writing Center offers many experiences to facilitate growth and enhance skills in all areas of development.

Physical Skills: enhance fine motor skills, develop visual discrimination, and develop eye-hand coordination.

Social/Emotional Skills: allow for the expression of feelings and emotions, develop appreciation for the writing of others, and promote cooperation, teamwork, sharing and collaboration.

Language Skills: increase oral communication skills and vocabulary, develop spelling, phonetic skills, understanding of the purposes of writing, and extend reading skills.

Intellectual Skills: develop thinking, reasoning, questioning, creativity and imagination, and promote problem solving skills.

Points to Remember

- Establish the center with clearly defined boundaries.
- Model the appropriate use of materials.
- Provide a variety of real-life, purposeful, writing materials.
- Add additional items and props to enhance writing and the current theme.
- Provide a place to display children's writing.
- Participate when invited and model writing. Encourage children to read what they are writing to you or others.
- Use labels and pictures to show where items belong to facilitate clean up.
- Create a literacy-rich center with word cards, word walls, dictionaries, and appropriate books.
- Keep materials in good working order, such as replacing dried-out markers.
- Enlist the help of adult volunteers to help with publishing tasks.

Suggested Writing Center Materials

Pencils	Sand and salt trays
Pens	Word wall
Chalk and chalkboard	Class list of names
Magic slates	Alphabet strips
Acetate sheets	Date stamps
Stapler	Computer
Paste or glue	Table or desks
Sharpener	Number stamps
Stationary	Journals
Colored pencils	Writing prompts
Crayons	Props for office play, card shop, and post office
Alphabet stamps	Print materials from doctors' or dentists' offices
Letter and design stencils	Dry erase board and markers
Hole punch	Chart tablets
Tape	Easel
Envelopes and cards	Notebooks
Markers	Sticky notes
Stamp pads	Folders
Index cards	Labels/stickers
Scissors	Yarn
Old magazines	Pipe cleaners
Alphabet charts	Adding machine tape
Book binding materials	Macaroni and spaghetti
Picture dictionaries	Highlighters
Paper	Picture prompts
Mailbox	Word search

Translations and Keys

UNIT 1　Child Rights 儿童权利

Translation of English Proficiency

儿童早期发展方案应该是什么样的？

儿童早期发展方案不仅是关于儿童的，还涉及对儿童成长环境的影响。方案应以家庭、社区和社会中已有的优势为基础来制定。同时，方案还应有利于逐步增强儿童的以下优势：

• 身体优势：如为母亲提供产前护理和营养，为儿童提供适当的营养；免疫；适当的住所；清洁的水；良好的环境卫生和个人卫生；发展粗大运动和精细运动技能的机会和鼓励。

• 智力优势：如语言习得和对故事的接触；激励儿童探索和好奇的活动；对数字、颜色、维度等基本概念的理解；鼓励创造性和批判性思维。

• 社交优势：如了解自己的身份，了解家庭关系和邻里关系；按照社会公认的准则与同伴及他人相处；获得良好的沟通能力，能够进行合作。

• 道德和情感优势：如拥有稳定的人际关系，爱，情感和安全感；理解家庭和社会的信仰体系；了解什么是明智的，什么是不明智的；成为一个批判思考者；逐渐获得并加强自我保护能力。

《公约》将发展视为一个持续的过程，即个体儿童及其固有的特性与当前以及更大的环境之间的互动过程，从而导致其能力和成熟度的不断变化……儿童是一个积极的参与者，而不是一块被操纵的空白石板。即使是最年幼的儿童也能沟通，作为成年人，我们的任务是鼓励和帮助他们发展自己的优势和技能……

……有许多选择和方法。有一些方面需要强调，如那些支持家长和家庭而不是取代他们的方案的重要性；如培训来自当地社区的人员实施儿童早期活动，而不是坚持认为所有人员都要有专业资质；如社区、家长和儿童参与其方案和活动的决策……

在许多国家，儿童早期发展方案已经启动……或由民间社会组织实施……政府的作用是创造一个（法律、政策、社会）环境，允许和鼓励幼儿及其家庭的健康发展……

其目的是确立能够确保所有幼儿都有机会最大限度发挥其先天潜能的可持续方案和服务……这是我们的集体责任。儿童不能等。

Keys to Unit Practice

1. Read aloud the phonemes and fill out the form.

Vowels 元音（20个）			Consonants 辅音（28个）		
单元音	前元音	[i:] [ɪ] [e] [æ]	爆破音	清辅音	[p] [t] [k]
				浊辅音	[b] [d] [g]

续表

	Vowels 元音（20个）			Consonants 辅音（28个）		
单元音	中元音	[ɜ:] [ə] [ʌ]		摩擦音	清辅音	[f] [θ] [s] [ʃ] [h]
					浊辅音	[v] [ð] [z] [ʒ] [r]
	后元音	[ɑ:] [ɒ] [ɔ:] [u] [u:]		鼻辅音		[m] [n] [ŋ]
双元音	合口双元音	[eɪ] [aɪ] [ɔɪ] [au] [əu]		破擦音	清辅音	[tʃ] [tr] [ts]
					浊辅音	[dʒ] [dr] [dz]
				舌边音		[l]
	集中双元音	[iə] [eə] [uə]		半元音		[w] [j]

2. Put the school languages into English.

　　早上好，宝贝！ Good morning, sweetie!

　　你今天看起来很棒！ You look great, today!

　　快进来！把书包放下。Come on in! Leave your schoolbag.

　　你有没有想我们？ Did you miss us?

　　今天就到这里了。下课！ That's all for today. Class dismissed.

　　你们今天过得开心吗？Were you happy today?

　　把你们的事情做完。Get your things done up.

　　请把书包带走。Take your schoolbag with you.

　　周一见！明天见！ See you Monday! See you tomorrow!

3. Put the following phrases and sentences into Chinese.

　　（1）语言习得

　　（2）听故事

　　（3）按照社会公认的准则与同伴和他人互动

　　（4）即使是最年幼的孩子也能交流。

　　（5）作为成年人，我们的任务是鼓励和帮助他们发展自己的能力和技能。

　　（6）社区、家长和儿童参与其方案和活动的决策。

4. Match the sentences with conversion words and the type of conversion.

v. → n.	We will try our best to **better** our living.
adj. → n.	Murder will **out**.
n. → v.	I think we'd better finish the **talk** now.
adj. → v.	We don't belong to the **rich**, but we don't belong to the **poor** either.
adv. → v.	The girl in **black** appears very beautiful.
The + adj.	**Hand** in your papers, please.

5. Chose the best answer to complete the sentences.

　　（1）D。第一空 the front door 表示"前门"，是特指；第二空表示"一种奇异的景象"，是泛指，用 a。

Translations and Keys

（2）C。句意：在交流中，微笑是友好和公开态度的明显象征。a sign of 表示"一种……的象征"，故第一个空填 a；attitude 为可数名词，friendly 和 open 并列，修饰 attitude。故选 C 项。

（3）B。第一空考查不定冠词表示泛指的用法，这里要表达"每年"之意，所以用不定冠词 a；第二空考查固定结构：by+the+ 具体计量单位，意思是"按照，依照"，by the week "按周计算"。

（4）B。emotion "情感"；principle "原理，原则"；regulation "管理；规则"；opinion "观点"。句意：无论如何，我不能欺骗他，那违背了我的处事原则。故选 B 项。

（5）B。result "结果"；cause "原因，理由"，常与介词 of 搭配，表示"……的原因"；warning "警告，警报，先兆"；reflection "反应，反射"。由空前的"缺少生态环保的习惯"与空后的 of global climate change 可推知，此处应用 cause 表示"全球气候变化的原因"。句意：公众缺少生态环保的习惯被认为是全球气候变化的一个主要原因。故选 B 项。

（6）D。 point 作为名词在句中的意思是"意义"。What's the point of ...? 表示"……有什么意义？" A 项"同情，怜悯"；B 项"主题"；C 项"物体；目标，对象；宾语"。

（7）C。out of one's reach 或 beyond one's reach 表示"在某人够不着的地方或力所不能及的范围"。句意：记住：把这些像刀子一样危险的东西放在孩子们够不着的地方。

（8）D。anger "生气；愤怒"；rudeness "粗鲁；无礼"；regret "后悔；遗憾"；panic "惊慌；惊恐"。句意："汤米，快跑，房子着火了！"母亲大声喊着，声音中透着明显的惊慌。根据句意，D 项正确。

Translation of Extended Reading

关于联合国儿童基金会

UNICEF 是联合国儿童基金会。我们在联合国大会上的使命就是帮助世界各地的儿童实现他们生存、发展、保护和参与的权利。联合国儿童基金会在 190 个国家和地区工作，以保护每个儿童的权利。联合国儿童基金会已经花了 70 年的时间来改善儿童及其家庭的生活。保护儿童的终身权利需要全球性的参与，旨在产生结果并理解其效果。联合国儿童基金会所做的每一件事都是为了促进每个儿童的权利和福祉。我们与我们的合作伙伴一道，在 190 个国家和地区开展工作，将这一承诺转化为实际行动，将特别努力的重点放在最易受伤害和被排斥的儿童身上，造福于世界各地的全体儿童。

2016 年世界儿童状况

2016 年世界儿童状况：每个儿童机会均等

每个儿童都有保持健康、受教育和受保护的权利，每个社会都与扩大儿童生存的机会利害攸关。 然而，在世界各地，除了国家、性别或出生环境之外，数百万的儿童被平白无故地剥夺公平的机会。"2016 年世界儿童状况"认为，处境最不利的儿童的进步不仅是道义上的，也是战略上的当务之急。 股份持有者要做出明确的选择：为加速落后儿童的进步而投资，不然到 2030 年要面临世界更加严重分裂的后果。在新的发展议程开始时，报告以一系列帮助制定走向更公平世界的建议而结束。

教育是获得机会的关键

联合国儿童基金会认为，无论是在发展中国家，还是国家处于冲突和危机中，优质教育是所有儿童的权利。

生命的初期对儿童的未来有深远的影响。当儿童在安全和激励的环境中被关爱、滋养和照顾时，他们就会发展出他们所需要的技能来拥抱机遇并从逆境中恢复技能。但在中低收入国家，近43%5岁以下的儿童没有得到所需的营养、保护和激励。这便削弱了儿童的潜力和整个社会的可持续增长。

好消息是：幼儿期显现出一个无与伦比的机会之窗，使儿童的生活与众不同。在适当的时间采取适当的干预措施可以克服不利因素，促进儿童的发展。

在世界各地，联合国儿童基金会的早期儿童发展方案提供了综合营养、保护和刺激以及支持父母、照护者和社区的干预措施，以帮助弱势儿童在生活中获得公平的开始。

配图1（王源被任命为联合国儿童基金会青年教育使者，将支持推广为每个儿童提供优质教育。）

北京，2017年6月28日——中国知名歌手、演员、流行乐队TFBOYS的成员，王源今天被联合国儿童基金会（UNICEF）任命为特别教育使者。

配图2（联合国儿童基金会中国代理代表道格拉斯·诺布尔（Douglas Noble）博士和中国知名歌手、演员、流行乐队TFBOYS成员王源于2017年6月28日在联合国儿童基金会北京办事处的一次活动中展示其共同签署的联合国儿童基金会特别教育顾问委托书。）

"我非常自豪地作为特别教育使者加入中国的联合国儿童基金会，这不仅是一种荣誉，也是一种责任。从今天起，我将更加积极地推动中国儿童的教育和发展，尽我所能做更多的实际工作。教育是一项权利；我们不应该让它成为一种特权。让我们努力让教育在未来变得更好。"王源在联合国儿童基金会北京办事处的宣布仪式上说。

联合国儿童基金会与中国政府合作，为中国所有儿童推广和支持优质教育。与合作伙伴一道，在中国偏远和贫困地区实施"儿童友好学校"模式。"儿童友好学校"是为儿童的最大利益而设计的。联合国儿童基金会认为，无论是谁，无论他们来自中国的哪个地区，他们都有接受优质教育的权利。

"我非常高兴地欢迎王源成为联合国儿童基金会中国的特别教育使者，"联合国儿童基金会中国代理代表道格拉斯·诺布尔博士说。"我们很感谢王源加入我们，努力来推动每一名儿童的优质教育。我们期待与我们的合作伙伴，以及所有辛勤工作的老师和学生的持续合作，以促进、保护和实现中国所有儿童的权利。"

王源将访问由联合国儿童基金会支持的在中国偏远农村社区的"儿童友好学校"项目，支持提高认识方案，并出席重大公开活动。

配图3（中国著名歌手、演员、流行乐队TFBOYS成员王源，于2017年6月28日在联合国儿童基金会中国北京办事处举行的任命他为"联合国儿童基金会特别教育使者"活动之后，与来自北京郊区的一所小学的10位小学生分享了他对优质教育的看法。）

要了解联合国儿童基金会及其工作的更多信息：

访问：http://www.unicef.org

访问UNICEF中国网站：http://www.unicef.cn

关注我们的新浪微博：http://weibo.com/unicefchina

微信：unicefchina

Translations and Keys

UNIT 2 Early Years Development 儿童早期发展

Translation of English Proficiency

早期开发框架

边学边玩耍

儿童通过玩耍成长和发展。低龄儿童,尤其是婴儿和幼儿,用他们的五种感官去探索世界。他们利用他们的视觉、嗅觉、触觉、听觉和味觉来了解周围的环境、物体和人。不同类型的游戏可以在不同的方面,如生理上、语言上、认知上、社交上和情感上促进儿童的发展。

玩耍时间不只是玩玩具的时间。玩耍涉及人、物体或运动。一切的一切,从摇摇铃、推车,到吹泡泡、唱歌、在浴缸里玩水、在房间里互相追逐、假扮不同的人物,都可算作玩耍。通过玩耍,幼儿能够学会结交朋友、合作、交流、解决问题,并能展示出许多其他的智力、情感和社交行为。他们成为狂热的探险家、发现者和意义建构者。

玩耍对儿童发展的影响是整体性和全方位的。玩耍的类型包括:物体游戏、感觉运动、社交游戏和表演游戏。幼儿需要自由和空间来玩耍,通过多种活动来运动和练习他们的新技能。他们可以从事不同类型的活动,这些活动需要不同的动作——行走、翻滚、蹦跳、爬行、攀爬、跳跃、平衡甚至是机动弯曲。这些运动活动也可以包括玩具、材料和设备。大型轻量的积木可以让幼儿在他们四周搬运和搭建结构时练习粗大运动技能,而球则是多功能的,可以用来踢、投、接和滚。

社交和表演游戏

表演游戏可以帮助儿童了解自己和与之相关的周围世界。当儿童进行表演或想象性的游戏时,他们可以学会协商不同的情境和角色,表达他们的情感和想法,发展友谊,创造性地思考,解决问题,发展粗大和精细的运动技能,并练习口头表达。

在初期的表演游戏中,幼儿通常把他们的游戏集中在对他们来说熟悉而有意义的经历上。他们经常模仿成人的行为,可能用真实的或逼真的物体作为道具,装扮、烹饪和摇动婴儿。然而,当儿童发展并开始获得象征性思考的能力时,他们就更善于用言语和行动代替真实的物体。年龄较大的儿童可能承担不同的社会角色,如妈妈、爸爸、婴儿、医生、教师等。

保教人员可以通过在表演区配备多种多样道具的方式来创造幼儿主导的、自发性的表演游戏机会。其中一些是毛绒玩具、洋娃娃、汽车、电话、道具服装、镜子、炉灶、锅碗瓢盆和家具。定期轮换道具,以保持和激发孩子们的兴趣。

Keys to Unit Practice

2. Write down the letters which sound as follows.

[æ] Aa   [k] Cc/Kk   [e] Ee   [dʒ] Jj   [ʌ] Uu
[kw] Qq   [ɪ] Ii/Yy   [ks] Xx   [j][ɪ] Yy [ɒ] Oo

3. Put the school languages into English.

我们来点名。Let's call the roll./Let's have a roll call.

听到名字请回答"到"。Say "here"/"I'm here." when your name is called.

今天星期几？What day is today?

我们来做律动吧！Let's do the rhyme.

和着音乐用手打拍子。Beat time to the music with your hands.

跟我一起做动作。Follow me and act with the music.

4. Put the following sentences into Chinese.

（1）儿童通过玩耍成长和发展。

（2）幼儿用他们的五种感观探索世界。

（3）玩耍时间不只是玩玩具的时间。

（4）玩耍的类型包括：物体游戏、感觉游戏、社交游戏和表演游戏。

（5）定期轮换道具，保持和激发幼儿的兴趣。

5. Read the words and name them.

impossible 不可能的　　　unpleasant 不高兴的　　　disorder 混乱的
minibus 小型公交车　　　overwork 过度劳累　　　pre-school 学前
kilogram 千克　　　　　　nonstop 直达的　　　　　mislead 误导
anti-war 反战争　　　　　bilingual 双语的　　　　recall 唤回/回忆

6. Chose the best answer to complete the sentences.

（1）C。句意：你能借给我一些钱吗？在请求疑问句中要用肯定形式，因此应该选 some。

（2）C。这里句中有 only，一般情况下，当 little, few 前面用 only/just 修饰时，必须用肯定形式。

（3）D。句意：那些来自乡村的人，请填写一下这张表格。这里是定语从句，all 作先行词时，关系代词只能用 that；anyone 作先行词时，谓语动词要用单数形式，因此不正确。在句中，一般用 that 来代替，这里是复数，因此应该选择 those。

（4）D。句意：她昨天去湖里游泳了，我也打算今天下午去游泳。这里是指做一样的事情，用代词 the same。

（5）A。句意：街道的两边都有高的建筑物。这里是 side 因此是每一边，两旁，因此用 either。

（6）A。句意：一个人必须尽他所能来服务人民。因此应选 A。

（7）B。这里指的是"我没有"，杂志不是人，因此排除 C，neither 和 no 不能单独使用，因此应该用 none。

（8）A。两个孩子都应该是 both of the children，这里 of 可以省略，因此选 A。

（9）C。这里考查的是"one ... the other (three, two...)"。句意：那四本书，其中一本是一个年轻的作家写的，其余的三本是一个年长的作家写的。因此选 C。

（10）D。of 是介词，其后应该加宾语，因此选择 us，这里 Bob, Tom and ___ 是 us 的同位语，us 已经使用宾语了，因此第 2 个空也要用宾格形式 me。

Translations and Keys

Translation of Extended Reading

表演游戏中心

幼儿热衷假装的模仿性活动。表演游戏中心让儿童有机会表演出他们的真实世界。他们可以体验不同的角色，表达情感，模仿周围人的行为和性格特征。这是一个最具创造性、最自然、最具参与性的地方。表演游戏中心的开放性让每个儿童都能在自己的发展水平上取得成功。

> **儿童发展目标**
>
> 戏剧表演游戏中心提供许多经历，以促进成长和提高所有发展领域的技能。
>
> **身体技能**：发展精细运动技能，增强粗大运动发展，并发展视觉辨别与手眼协调能力。
>
> **社交/情感技能**：提供一种表达情感和情绪的方法；开发对自我、家庭和社会的认识；促进合作，与他人共事，分享和依次轮流。
>
> **语言技能**：增加口语沟通能力，扩展和增强词汇量，增强粗大运动发展，开发假装读写能力。
>
> **智力技能**：发展创造力和想象力，提升解决问题的能力，扩展象征性物件的使用和抽象思维的能力。

需要记住的几点：

- 将表演游戏中心安置在其他有噪声的活动区域旁边。
- 在该区域的三面创建边界，以存留材料。
- 推出时，只在表演游戏中心放置少量物品。
- 添加额外的物品和道具以增强游戏和当前的主题。
- 保持道具清洁和维修良好。
- 使用标签和图片来表明物品属于哪里，便于清理。
- 通过坐或跪的方式跟儿童在同一水平线（高度）互动。
- 受到邀请时要参与表演并做示范表演。鼓励儿童谈论他们正在做的事情。
- 允许孩子自主解决矛盾。
- 为小件物品、钩子或衣架提供带小标签的箱子或篮子。
- 提供读写机会，如书籍和写作用具。

建议表演游戏中心教具材料投放

杯子	银器
餐具	炊具
桌子和椅子	厨房家具
厨房用品	围裙
花瓶和花	塑料制食品
空食品箱	擦盘子毛巾
扫帚和簸箕	腰带、鞋子
电话和电话簿	生活家具

道具服装	儿童安全工具带，工具
钱包	杂志
娃娃和婴儿用品	手提箱
化妆品	手包
没有电线的旧吹风机	便笺和铅笔
全身镜	多文化服装和材料
午餐盒	手机

道具箱的想法

提供丰富的表演游戏和道具箱，作为培养技能和学习概念的机会。

沙滩
- 毯子
- 野餐篮子
- 沙滩伞
- 太阳镜
- 沙滩球
- 假装的防晒乳液
- 沙滩巾
- 铲斗和铲子
- 贝壳
- 潜水通气管
- 蛙鞋
- 人字拖

消防队员
- 黄色橡胶雨衣
- 旧的真空软管
- 消防汽笛
- 活梯
- 电话
- 手电筒
- 靴子
- 消防安全宣传海报
- 手套
- 婴儿玩偶（救援用）
- 对讲机
- 防火帽

餐厅
- 台布
- 餐巾
- 餐具
- 用食品图片制作的菜单
- 菜
- 围裙
- 托盘
- 道具食品
- 帽子
- 饭店的标志
- 点餐笺/铅笔

邮局
- 信封
- 邮票（密封/贴纸）
- 行李袋
- 邮递员帽子
- 收银机
- 旧的蓝衬衫
- 贴纸
- 打孔机
- 明信片
- 秤
- 邮箱
- 钢笔
- 铅笔
- 纸
- 垃圾邮件
- 箱子
- 包裹

支票簿
行事历
道具桌子

食杂店
道具食品
蛋盒
结账区
道具钱
购物车或篮子
围裙
纸袋
收银机或扫描仪
销售传单
手包和钱包
塑料制水果/蔬菜
优惠券

警察
写票笺
停止的标志牌
小夹板
警察帽
车牌
汽笛
方向盘
黑带
911 标志
蓝色衬衫
对讲机
徽章

银行
道具钱
银行存折
添加机器/计算器
橡皮图章/印台
出纳窗口
存款单/支票
现金箱
纸/笔

硬币卷
放大镜
报纸

面包店
新鲜玩具面团
擀面杖
围裙
烤箱手套
烤盘
厨师帽
松饼罐
蛋糕盘
蛋糕装饰
点菜笺
量匙
烘焙食品图片
搅拌碗
勺子
食谱
饼干模具
面粉筛
烹饪菜谱

兽医
毛绒动物玩具
纱布
外科口罩
动物小册子
棉花球
塑胶手套
玩具钱
无针注射器
检查台
空药瓶
宠物刷
白大褂
宠物便携包
放大镜

UNIT 3 The Benefits of Playgrounds 操场的益处

Translation of English Proficiency

为 0~5 岁儿童提供操场的益处

操场为孩子们提供关键和重要的玩耍的机会。有大量研究表明，玩耍与大脑发育，运动技能和社交能力之间存在明显的联系。所有的学习——不管是情感上、社交上、运动上还是认知上——都是由玩耍的乐趣来加速、促进和助力的。促进操场提供不同类型的游戏对于儿童的认知、情感、身体和社会发展都至关重要。与在沙斯塔县安装方法类似的，促进成长的操场和游戏设备更具体的做法描述如下：

玩耍和自由玩耍

什么是玩耍？玩耍就是单纯的玩乐，是儿童的自发活动。玩耍包括许多内容。它可以通过身体（跑步、跳跃、跳舞）、心灵（幻想游戏）、道具（搭积木、推玩具）和语言（笑话、唱歌）来完成。玩耍由好奇心激发和驱使。玩耍开始简单，随着儿童的成长而变得越来越复杂。

操场提供自由玩耍的机会。自由玩耍不同于有条理的课间休息玩耍或有组织的运动和比赛。操场自由玩耍在广泛的结构和空间支持下，可以让儿童以任何他们选择的方式来玩耍。自由玩耍可以让儿童根据自己的自然倾向进行探索，可以让他们相互学习，并与广泛的年龄层的儿童进行互动。

语言发展、智力和社交技能

玩耍是想象力、智力和语言发展的主要手段。操场将儿童与同伴一起玩耍的机会最大化。与同伴之间的互动可以让儿童表达想法和感受，并发展口语能力。游乐设施促进社交游戏的发展，因为它们为儿童提供了聚集和交流的场所。通过玩耍的行为，他们可以学会社交和文化的规则，体验各种各样的情绪，并探索社会共享的符号系统。通过玩耍，他们也可以经过身心反复试错、与环境和同伴的互动，来学会区分相关信息和不相关信息的能力。简而言之，操场的缺乏会增加儿童的被动性。

一个说明在操场上自由玩耍能帮助社会技能发展的例子，可以在"游戏"的自发性创造中看到。无论是捉人游戏，抑或是将游乐设施做成城堡，让儿童自己分配角色（守卫、国王、皇后等）的幻想游戏，都需要同伴的互动来建立"游戏规则"并开始游戏。儿童在社交环境中学习协商、妥协、共同合作，并且控制自己，容忍挫折，因为不遵守自创的"规则"，他们就不能顺利地继续与同伴一起玩耍。将不同的操场元素连接在一起的模块化结构通过配备不同类型的互动来提供社会化的机会——独自一人的角落；两三个孩子的僻静处；成人、儿童一对一互动的场所和小群体的场所。

Keys to Unit Practice

1. Read aloud and write down the following words according to the phonics.

[wɔnt] want   [truː] true   [ˈbɪzi] busy
[aɪs] ice   [ˈprɪti] pretty   [ˈjuːnɪt] unit

Translations and Keys

2. Put the school languages into English.

排队！站成一排！ Line up, please./ Make one line.

不要推搡，小心脚下！ No pushing. Watch your steps.

站直！稍息！立正！报数！ Stand straight. At ease. Attention. Let's count off.

齐步走！向左转！向右转！ Quick time, march. Turn left. Turn right.

向前看齐！手放下！ Arms out. Arms in.

向前走，不要停！ Go ahead. Keep going.

3. Put the following phrases and sentences into Chinese.

（1）操场为儿童玩耍提供了关键和重要的玩耍的机会。

（2）玩耍是想象力、智力和语言发展的主要手段。

（3）儿童学习谈判、妥协、共同合作，并且控制自己。

（4）有条理的课间休息玩耍或有组织的运动和游戏

（5）玩耍开始简单，随着儿童的成长而变得越来越复杂。

4. Read the derived words and name them.

boredom 无聊　　　　handful 一把　　　　membership 会员

examination 检查；考试　careless 粗心的　　regularity 规律性

selfishness 自私　　　removal 去除/移走　　employee 雇员

5. Chose the best answer to complete the sentences.

（1）C。考查基数词和不可数名词的搭配问题。句意：先生，您想要点什么？两瓶汽水。pop 是不可数名词，two 后的名词应该用复数形式，故选 C。当数词和不可数名词搭配时，应用"数词 + 可数名词 +of+ 中心词 (不可数名词)"的结构。在这个结构中，如果这个数词大于 1，后面的可数名词要用复数形式。

（2）D。句意：许多女孩参加《快乐女生》的比赛，但是仅有少数人能够成功。million 后面跟 of 的时候一定要用复数形式，表示"成千上万的，许多的"。

（3）B。考查分数的表达和主谓一致。句意：四分之三的地球表面被海洋覆盖。当分子大于 1 时，分母用序数词的复数形式。"四分之三的地球表面"看作一个整体故动词用第三人称单数形式。

（4）D。考查序数词作定语。句意：在我十五岁生日的时候，我得到了一辆漂亮的自行车，我非常喜欢它。根据句意可知，是第十五个生日，序数词作定语时，其前要加 the 或形容词性的物主代词。

（5）C。第一空是定语从句 the boy 指人，故用关系代词 who；第二空可根据句意知道是他的第九个生日，故选 C。句意："你认识坐彼得附近的那个男孩吗？""是的，他是彼得的朋友，他们正在庆贺他的第九个生日。"

（6）B。根据句意可知，空白处要用序数词，序数词前有物主代词时，不用再加 the，故选 B。句意：在我九岁生日时，我得到了一份很棒的礼物。

（7）C。基数词之后用 million 的单数形式，再根据句意可知，是第六十个儿童节，故选 C。句意：你看了电视上的中央新闻吗？是的，在第 60 个儿童节时，数百万名儿童过得很快乐。

（8）C。基数词之后用 hundred 的单数形式，hundred 的复数形式与 of 连用，故选 C。句意：附近已经植了数百棵树，因此空气非常新鲜。

（9）A。当分子大于 1 时，分母用复数形式，这样可排除 B 和 C，land 是不可数名词，谓语动词用单数形式，故选 A。句意：那个地区五分之二的陆地被树和草所覆盖。

（10）C。根据前面的 four times 可知，要试第 5 次。句意：虽然我失败了 4 次，但我的爸爸鼓励我尝试第 5 次。

Translation of Extended Reading

数学中心

当数学中心配备各种各样的实物材料时，很容易让学生参与到数字、测量和解决问题中去。这为探索数学概念、实践新技能和应用他们掌握的技能打下了坚实的基础。

儿童发展目标

数学中心为促进发展和提高所有发展领域的技能提供很多经历。

身体技能： 加强精细运动的控制，改善眼手协调能力。

社交/情感技能： 培养自我控制能力，增强毅力和信心，通过分享材料和共同解决问题来加强合作。

语言技能： 引入数学语言，提高提出问题和讲解答案的能力。

智力技能： 引入并改进整理、匹配、归类、排序、形成模式、一一对应、背诵计数（唱数）、数字组合、问题的解决。

需要记住的几点：

- 每次推出一种新的数学材料。
- 示范适当的使用、护理和清理程序。
- 在要求学生做一项具体任务之前，让他们自由地探索材料。
- 让学生使用各种数学材料来学习同样的技能或概念。
- 找到有趣而不同寻常的数学材料。
- 使数学有意义。例如：为商店做些改变，为烹饪做测量，把零食分成等份或是绘制一个班级郊游的选项图。
- 提供多种方法让学生记录他们在数学中心所做的工作：绘图、图表、图形、书籍、橡皮图章、贴纸或实物。
- 当学生在中心活动时，观察和倾听他们，这样可以深刻了解他们开始形成的数字概念。
- 在游戏中通过引入数学语言来拓展学生活动。

建议数学中心教具材料投放

可收藏的教具：纽扣、钥匙、彩色面团、贝壳、石块、面包标签、彩色回形针、豆子、牙签

Translations and Keys

塑料筹码	冰块托盘
图案块	形状模板和书写用品
图案卡	线轴
1英寸彩色立方体	衣夹
1英寸木立方体	吸管
彩色瓷砖	数模版
属性积木	数字邮票和便笺
多重立方体	数字线
拼花积木	计算器
分类盘/碗	分类容器
测量仪器，如标尺、码尺、量杯、量勺	缸
天平秤和用来称重的东西	罐
小钉板和钉	桶
串珠	拉链密封袋
游戏和拼图	贴纸
骰子和旋转器	扑克牌
地板图	创建模式用的计数器卷带
磁板	收银机
带磁性的图形和数字	价格标签
个人标记板和黑板	优惠券
时钟	数学大书
玩钱	统计图表
橡皮图章	颜色词图
与数学相关的书籍、歌曲、诗歌、图表或海报	形状图
	游戏
计时器	定义空间的呼啦圈
多米诺骨牌	蛋盒
日历	笔记本
钥匙	盘垫
珠子	托盘
螺母、螺栓、垫圈或螺丝	午餐袋或礼品袋
回形针	公告板

UNIT 4　Learning Environment 1 学习环境（一）

Translation of English Proficiency

儿童早期学习环境

学习环境是一种重要而强大的教学工具。早教老师的大部分工作都是在幼儿到达之前完成的。如果环境是建立在对儿童如何学习和发展的认知基础上的，那么它就能积极地支持教学和学习。对学生行为表现感到吃力的老师应该认真评估每天的课程表、教室布置、每个学习中心的教具材料以及课程设置。

最佳范例

在创造一个积极的儿童早期环境时，应注意以下做法：
- 教室应该安排好，用学习材料来促进学生的探索。
- 学习材料应该是具体的，并且与幼儿自身的生活经历有关（开放式的但有目的的）。
- 教室环境应该设置成可供选择的。
- 应该计划好学习经历，以便在获得新技能的小群体环境中，能够存在教师发起或儿童发起的机会。
- 课程表应体现活跃的和安静的学习活动，大组、小组和个体的学习时间，老师指导的和幼儿发起的活动以及室内和室外活动。

课程表

课程表对每天的基本结构至关重要。一惯性能使幼儿有安全感，让他们有信心和自由去探索课堂环境。尽管一惯性很重要，但保持灵活性也是必要的。如果幼儿对某个活动或讨论的话题特别感兴趣，就需要安排额外的时间。

学年初，大组、小组活动的计划时间较短。随着这一年时间的推移，学习中心的时间将是一天中较少的一部分。大组活动数量减少，但时间通常会延长。儿童早期教育／家庭教育网站（http://sde.state.ok.us）下的"有用的表格"链接提供了课程表的样本。

一个精心设计的课程表将会：
- 优先考虑幼儿与同伴、老师和学习材料互动的需要。
- 给幼儿留有足够的时间发起并完成活动，参与创造性运动和自我表现。
- 交替安排活跃的与活动量小的学习时段，而不是长时间久坐不动。
- 尊重幼儿适当休息或适当活动的需要，不能让学习时间的质量打折扣。
- 体现整合教学，而不是以学科来划分课堂时间。
- 提供充足的时间让幼儿通过以学习中心为基础的课程来学习。
- 安排好活动之间或课堂之间的顺利转换，教师应把这些转换当成学习的时间。
- 为幼儿提供与小组分享的机会，并为他们小小的成就感到骄傲。
- 安排合作计划的时间，使幼儿在课堂学习活动中拥有自主权。

Translations and Keys

转换

转换是从一个活动转移到另一个活动的过程。这对幼儿来说常常是有困难的。教师必须用"吸引注意力妙法"来提示这种变化，如歌曲、信号、手指游戏、儿歌、游戏和木偶。利用转换活动的教师将会拥有安静且有组织的课堂和快乐、合作的儿童。如果使用得当，这些转换活动可以成为施教时刻。关于转换活动的例子，请访问早期儿童（家庭）教育网站：http://sde.state.ok.us，点击页面下的"有用的表格"链接。

顺利转换的有用提示
- 在下次活动前给予足够的预警。
- 尽量严格遵守每天的课程表。当幼儿知道该做什么和会发生什么时，他们就能在日常学习中成长。灵活性意味着缩短或延长一天中的某一部分时间，而不是完全改变课程表。一定要在"特殊情况"发生之前让幼儿做好准备。
- 要制定周密的计划。活动前收集材料。认真考量每一次转换，并将转换活动纳入每日计划中。
- 将转换信号与具体的活动联系起来。
- 使用歌曲和手指游戏。
- 将转换活动整理成笔记或汇总到一个档案盒里。

集中活动时间

集中活动时间是一天中最重要的时刻之一。在这期间，教师、助教和儿童作为一个团体聚在一起，在他们分享、学习、倾听和参与有意义的活动中发展信任和接纳。集中活动时间的模式应保持一年不变，这样儿童会因为预先了解后面要进行的活动而产生自信。集中活动时间为儿童提供在独立活动和小组活动中获得成功所必需的信息、技能、概念以及策略。

集中活动时间指南
- 集中活动时间的时长取决于儿童的年龄和发展阶段。 在学年初，集中活动时间可能只有 10~15 分钟。
- 为每次集中活动都制定明确的活动目标，并提前收集所有有用的素材。
- 设计平衡的活动，包括听、唱歌、讨论和运动。提供齐声回答和个人回答的机会。
- 将活动与儿童过去的经历和先前的知识联系起来。
- 让儿童成为决定一项活动成功与否的向导。根据儿童兴趣的指引来延长或缩短活动时间。

建议集中活动时间的活动内容
- 晨会
- 日历和天气
- 大声朗读
- 图片/词汇发展
- 韵律活动
- 解决问题的活动
- 园龄前幼儿（日托生）的音韵意识或幼儿园字母和单词墙活动

- 运动活动（歌曲、手指游戏、律动和游戏）
- 分组游戏
- 学生分享
- 班级会议
- 新概念导入
- 演讲嘉宾
- 示范教室教具材料的适当使用和保养
- 集中写作活动
- 重温课堂规则

Keys to Unit Practice

1. Read aloud and write down the following words according to the phonics.

[pleɪ]　play　　　　　[greɪt]　great　　　　　[bred]　bread
[θriː]　three　　　　['mʌŋki]　monkey　　　[njuː]　new

2. Put the school languages into English.

大家坐成圆圈。Everybody, please take a seat in a circle.

请注意！ May I have your attention?

我们来做沉默游戏。Let's play silence game.

圆圈时间不要玩耍。请遵守规则！ No playing during circle time. Behave yourself.

我喜欢杰瑞的坐姿。I like the way that Jerry is sitting.

请回到你的座位上。Please go back to your seat.

3. Put the following phrases and sentences into Chinese.

（1）评估每一个学习中心的每日课程表、教室布置、材料和课程设置。

（2）创造一个积极的儿童早期环境。

（3）课堂应该组织起来，以学习材料促进探究。

（4）学习材料应该是具体的，并且与儿童自己的生活经历有关（开放式但有目的的）。

（5）教室环境应设置成可选的。

4. Read the derived words and name them.

simple-minded　头脑简单的　　　useful　有用的　　　　　childish　幼稚的
wireless　无线的　　　　　　　 monkeylike　猴子般的　　drinkable　可饮用的
calmly　冷静地　　　　　　　　clockwise　顺时针的/地　　friendly　友好的

5. Chose the best answer to complete the sentences.

（1）C。由"限定词—数词—描绘词（大小、长短、形状、新旧、颜色）—性质+名词"的顺序可知，这里是"数词＋描绘词＋性质"的顺序，因此选C。

Translations and Keys

（2）A。几个形容词修饰一个名词，它们的排列顺序是：年龄、形状、大小、颜色、来源、质地、用途、国家＋名词，因此选 A。

（3）B。本题考查多个形容词的排序问题。一般与被修饰形容词关系密切的形容词靠近名词；如果几个形容词的重要性差不多，音节少的形容词在前，音节多的在后。在不能确定其顺序时，可参照：限定词＋数量（序数词在前，基数词在后）＋形状＋大小＋长短＋高低＋新旧＋颜色＋国籍＋材料＋名词，如 those ＋ three ＋ beautiful ＋ large ＋ square ＋old ＋ brown ＋ wood ＋ table，因此选 B。

（4）B。any 可修饰比较级，quite 修饰原级，well 的比较级为 better。

（5）C。much 可修饰比较级，因此 B、C 可选，但 easier 已是比较级，不需要 more，因此 C 为正确答案。

（6）D。本题是限定词＋形容词比较级＋名词的格式。

（7）D。句意：中国的天气比美国热。该句比较的是天气而不是国家，故 C 不能选。A 没有名词，后句成分不全，可排除。B 中的 one 常用来代替可数名词，而 that 可以代替不可数或抽象名词，因此选 D。

（8）C。句意：在引进新技术后，这个厂 1988 年生产的拖拉机是往年的两倍。表示倍数用"倍数＋as ＋形容词原形＋as ＋比较对象"结构，因此选 C。

（9）C。三者或三者以上进行比较应用最高级。

（10）A。在 so (such) ... that ... 的句型中，so 修饰形容词或副词，such 修饰名词。

Translation of Extended Reading

技术中心

技术中心是早期儿童教室环境的重要补充，前提是建立在具有对儿童发展的知识和对设备和现用软件的知识基础上。你的技术中心只会和技术中心的教具材料一样好，所以在购买设备前仔细考虑一下这个问题。成人互动是技术中心成功的关键。

儿童发展目标

为促进成长、提高全面发展的技能，技术中心提供了许多经验。

身体技能：通过控制键盘和鼠标，来跟踪屏幕和移动光标，以增强手眼协调和视觉感知，从而促进精细运动发育。

社交/情感技能：促进责任感、合作精神、与他人共事和坚持不懈。

语言技能：通过将文字与图片联系起来，增加词汇量和打印知识。

智力技能：通过观察键盘上发生的事情、遵循指示以及依靠所选软件等其他技能来开发因果关系。

需要记住的几点：

- 一次把电脑或其他技术介绍给一两个儿童。
- 观察儿童，这样你就知道如何与他们讨论和互动，以进一步提高他们的使用水平。

•问一些开放式的问题，而这些问题要集中在他们正在做的事情上。

•参考由高瞻课程教育研究基金会出版的、Warren Buckleitner 编写的《早期儿童软件调查》一书，来了解适用的软件。

•参考 Dodge 和 Colker 的《创新课程》，来了解关于建立一个技术中心的全面信息。

建议技术中心教具材料投放

电脑屏幕	光盘
鼠标	光盘播放器
硬盘驱动器	数字视频光盘
浪涌电压保护器	数字视频播放器
电脑桌	放大镜
充足的电源和电源插座	双筒望远镜
鼠标垫	电话
适用的软件程序	MP3 播放器
桌子	无线电
相机	扬声器
摄像机	标签制作器
磁带录音机	光秀道具
文字处理程序	计算器
班级网站	气象站
网页设计程序	温度计
教育视频游戏	电脑模拟时钟
电视机	数字时钟
视频播放器	手表

UNIT 5　Learning Environment II 学习环境（二）

Translation of English Proficiency

建立学习环境

　　教室的环境向学生传达了对他们的期望。教室环境应该传达独立和学习的乐趣。在早期教育课堂中，学习中心的使用是保证学生成功的关键因素。

教室布置

　　当计划在何处设立中心时，仔细看看你的教室，需要有三个基本的环境设置：一个是全班同学一起活动的地方，一个是学生独立活动的地方，另一个是由教师指导的小组活动场所。使用一幅教室的地图，用按比例剪下的家具和设备的图样来尝试不同的布置是很有帮助的。一旦布置好了你的教室并观察了在这个环境中的学生，就可能需要做一些调整以更好地适应学生的需求。

记住以下注意事项：

- 创建合理的通行模式，使学生可以轻松地从教室的一个区域移动到另一个区域，而不会打扰他人。
- 考虑固定物品的摆放，如水槽、嵌入式书架、铺地毯或瓷砖的地板及电源插座；要有效利用空间。
- 把安静和嘈杂的活动区域分开。
- 为集体活动提供宽阔的地面空间。
- 创建一个用于教师指导小组活动的空间。
- 提供个人活动的空间。
- 在学习中心附近存放适当的会被用到的材料和设备。

建议配备的学习中心

　　以下是早期教育课堂中常见的一组学习中心。关于中心活动区的讨论应包括建议投放的材料和设计的活动。

艺术中心	积木中心
文化中心	表演游戏中心
图书馆中心	音乐和运动中心
听力中心	烹饪中心
写作中心	计算机中心
数学中心	木工中心
科学和感官中心	

　　幼儿园龄前（日托生）的教室可能希望把语言、识字、数学和科学中心整合成一个大型游戏中心。

学习中心指南

　　学习中心材料的选择和布置应以促进参与、独立、决策和责任为目标。通过选择和使用每个中心提供的材料，学生们有很大的机会练习这些技能。为了确保学生和学习中心在课堂上的成功，建议遵循以下准则：
- 以讨论相关规则、材料的使用以及责任来介绍每一个学习中心。
- 可以使用轮转制度或自选制度安排学生进入中心。当使用轮转制度时，学生以一种有条不紊的方式穿行各个学习中心。当使用自选制度时，学生们自己穿行各个中心。
- 所有学习中心都有广泛的活动内容，以适应每个学生的兴趣和发展水平。
- 每一个中心的技能水平在一年中通过各种开放式的活动来提高。
- 每次都要为新的活动做示范。
- 用低矮的架子、地毯或胶带来标明中心边界。
- 在靠近学生使用点的矮架子上安排好材料，这样学生们就总是可以随手拿到各个中心的材料。
- 把小件物品安排在贴了标签的桶或篮子里，以便于清理。
- 利用符号来描述在每个中心活动时所学到的技能。
- 在架子上摆放图片、文字或物体的轮廓，以引导学生在完成活动时把材料放回原位。

教室

室外环境也可以是学习活动集中的室内教室的延伸。这样做就可以在你的教室里添加以下设备。
- 沙水台
- 栅栏或独立的画架（画可以看到的花）
- 带轮子的书车（在树荫下读书）
- 表演游戏的材料：
  - ——烧烤中心
  - ——野餐桌和篮子
  - ——帐篷
  - ——园艺中心
- 科学发现工具（放大镜、望远镜、蝴蝶网、昆虫捕捉设备）
- 木工材料
- 几乎所有带轮子的东西

Keys to Unit Practice

1. Read aloud and write down the following words according to the phonics.

   [ˈlaɪən] __lion__　　　　[piːs] __piece__　　　　[ˈdʒiːnɪəs] __genius__

   [ˈmɑːrɪəʊ] __Mario__　　[ˈkwaɪət] __quiet__　　[ˈkʊki] __cookie__

2. Put the school languages into English.

   我要讲一个故事。I'm going to tell a story./I'm going to share a story with you.
   看这幅图。Look at the picture.
   谁来试一下？Who wants to try?/Who wants to have a try?

Translations and Keys

请跟我读。Read after me./Say it after me.

有问题请举手。Raise/Put up your hands if you have any questions.

有人主动要做吗？ May I ask for a volunteer?/Any volunteers?

3. Put the following phrases into Chinese.

（1）教室（环境）布置

（2）创建学习环境

（3）一个让全班一起合作的地方

（4）一个让学生独立操作的地方

（5）一个教师指导小组活动的地方

（6）一个轮转系统或一个自选系统

（7）每次都要为新的活动做示范

4. Read the compounding words and name them.

ten-year-old 十岁的　　　　sleeping-pill 安眠药　　　　quick-charge 快速充电
takeaway 外卖　　　　　　　hand-made 手工制作的　　　world-famous 世界闻名的
income 收入　　　　　　　　newborn 新生儿　　　　　　greenhouse 温室

5. Decide the following sentences true (T) or false (F).

（1）We got to the top of the mountain in daybreak.　　　　　　　　　　　　（ × ）

　　　We got to the top of the mountain at daybreak.　　　　　　　　　　　（ √ ）

（2）By the end of next week, I will have finished this work.　　　　　　　　（ √ ）

　　　Till the end of next week, I will have finished this work.　　　　　　　（ × ）

（3）We visited the old man on Sunday afternoon.　　　　　　　　　　　　（ √ ）

　　　We visited the old man in Sunday afternoon.　　　　　　　　　　　　（ × ）

（4）Do you know the girl in white?　　　　　　　　　　　　　　　　　　（ √ ）

　　　Do you know the girl on white?　　　　　　　　　　　　　　　　　　（ × ）

（5）There is a beautiful bird on the tree.　　　　　　　　　　　　　　　　（ × ）

　　　There is a beautiful bird in the tree.　　　　　　　　　　　　　　　　（ √ ）

（6）School will begin on September 1st.　　　　　　　　　　　　　　　　（ √ ）

　　　School will begin in September 1st.　　　　　　　　　　　　　　　　（ × ）

（7）There is an old stone bridge above the river.　　　　　　　　　　　　（ × ）

　　　There is an old stone bridge over the river.　　　　　　　　　　　　（ √ ）

（8）I haven't seen you during the summer holidays.　　　　　　　　　　　（ × ）

　　　I haven't seen you since the beginning of the summer holidays.　　　（ √ ）

（9）On entering the classroom, I heard the good news.　　　　　　　　　（ √ ）

　　　At entering the classroom, I heard the good news.　　　　　　　　　（ × ）

（10）At the beginning of the book, there are some interesting stories.　　　（ √ ）

　　　In the beginning of the book, there are some interesting stories.　　　（ × ）

Translation of Extended Reading

户外环境

运动技能的发展对儿童的整个成长过程都至关重要。目前的研究表明，运动可以激活大脑并使大脑为学习做好准备。户外环境是发生这种现象的自然场所。精心规划户外活动是充分利用孩子运动和学习自然动机的好方法。

儿童发展目标

户外环境为促进发展和提高所有发展领域的技能提供了许多经验。

身体技能：增强大运动与手眼协调、平衡、力量、忍耐力和控制力。

社交/情感技能：培养合作、协商、轮流和角色扮演。

语言技能：促进词汇发展、方位词和交谈技能。

智力技能：通过沙水台活动加强整理、分类、创造力、想象力、问题解决、探索、发现、空间关系和对话。

建议户外环境材料投放

- 滑梯（适当高度）
- 爬行和隧道设备
- 卡车和汽车
- 跳绳
- 浇注和舀取材料
- 儿童大小的木桩
- 缓冲材料（卵石或沙子）
- 降落伞
- 游戏（抛圈或豆袋）
- 攀爬结构
- 骑行装备
- 推拉玩具
- 甬路
- 垃圾桶
- 树
- 阴凉或部分覆盖的游乐区
- 球
- 望远镜
- 沙子玩具
- 什锦球
- 低平衡木
- 呼啦圈
- 货车
- 滑板车
- 跷跷板
- 户外画架
- 桌子和长椅
- 沙水台
- 科学发现工具
- 花园和园艺工具
- 急救箱
- 人行道或坚硬、光滑的表面
- 人行道粉笔
- 表演游戏材料
- 水桶和油漆刷
- 排队区

安排

安排户外环境对于有效的规划至关重要。精心策划的玩耍空间可以使儿童的选择和独立最大化。教师必须不断评估户外区域的整体效能，并随时随地根据需要进行调整。在规划户外环境时，可以使用许多与室内环境规划相同的考虑因素。
- 空间足够大以容纳儿童和设备的数量。
- 可以从任何位置轻松监督儿童。
- 足够的设备可供使用，使儿童不必排队等待。
- 提供各种与年龄相适应的材料和设备。
- 配有储存棚子用于存放材料和设备。
- 日照处和阴凉处要平衡。
- 有很明确的跑步和骑乘玩具的道路。
- 游乐区用围栏围起，以免受交通影响。
- 厕所和饮水机方便使用。
- 适当考虑并满足每个儿童的具体需要。

安全

儿童对户外活动充满热情，所以安全规划至关重要。防止伤害最好的方法是预防。在你的安全计划中应包括以下内容：
- 提供持续监督。
- 在攀爬设备下提供足够的缓冲材料。
- 为每件设备提供足够的空间。
- 定期维护设备并上报任何破损或不安全的设备。
- 选择适合儿童智力、社交/情感和身体发育的设备和材料。
- 立即向相关的学校工作人员报告事故或危险情况。
- 教给儿童在紧急情况下迅速排好队并撤离游乐场的正确方法。

UNIT 6　Pre-school Music Education 学前音乐教育

Translation of English Proficiency

学前音乐教育

音乐的动作反应

在PME（学前音乐教育）中应用音乐的动作反应，为儿童提供了一种通过身体动作来理解和感知音乐的有用工具。课程中所呈现的歌曲几乎总是伴随着身体动作的。

音乐的动作反应可以看作是内化音乐的一种动感的表现方式。

动作活动成为"副耳"，使活动中声音的所有方面：音质、时长、强度、有声与无声及音色，都可以通过肌肉的张力和动作的能量输入来体验。空间和时间的动作体验本身可以唤起近、远、上、下、高、低的内隐概念，从而"组织进入节拍时间现象"，通过运动促进对音乐方面的回忆。因此，对音乐的动作反应可以被看作是学前儿童音乐理解力的指标。

儿童可以对音乐做出动作反应，是因为他们掌握一种时间表现形式。音乐运动的表现也意味着时间上的动作调节。"将动作与外部节奏同步"，这是音乐节拍的一个关键方面。

学前音乐教育

所有的PME（学前音乐教育）活动都要以对学前儿童音乐及总体发展的认识为基础。在活动中得到享受是一个重要的方面，因为儿童会因此而积极参与其中。根据杜威的说法，"享受（乐趣）本身不足以让一段经历有教育意义。"尽管这是一种含蓄的表达，但这正是音乐课程与随便的音乐游戏的区别所在。平均的PME课程包含每周10节、每节45分钟的课，课上要有8~10个儿童及其家长的参与。每堂课将准备10~12个活动。在每一课中，由于重复的重要性，只呈现2种新的活动。除了动作，通常这些歌曲还涉及音乐教具材料或玩具的使用。当关注音乐的发展时，我们可以看到，PME的音乐发展目标是广泛的：节奏感：节拍点、反应点；强弱力度感：大、小声；曲式感：有音乐与无音乐（无声），变奏；节拍感：快、慢；声音的形成：发声、共鸣；听音能力：专注，将注意力引向一个音源。这些音乐发展目标是由伴随着每首歌的动作活动来支持的。这些动作本身也描绘了歌曲的歌词。

有一个例子是"熊妈妈和熊宝宝"，这是一个节奏稳定的活动。

儿童可以踩着歌曲的节拍行走，让他们体验节奏，在歌曲重复几次之后，把节奏变快一些，让儿童体会节奏快与慢的差别。歌曲的中间，儿童可以抬起一条腿（体现歌词内容），这是一个反应的时间点，即音乐的节拍点。儿童需要注意在恰当的时间点抬起一条腿。重要的是他们必须预感到这一刻。因此，歌曲要重复至少5次，让儿童有时间学习这首歌，踩准时间点，将他们的动作与歌曲的节奏同步。这样，儿童就能建立起记忆；在一个特定的点，他们知道什么会到来。PME课程中，0~4岁儿童的歌曲比较短，只有一节。歌曲越长，就越难以把所有的东西都储存在记忆中，并预感在恰当的时机拍手、踩脚、表演。于是模仿就会发生。在这个框架中，区分节拍点（即踩准节拍点）和模仿是很重要的。为了踩准点，你需要预测好时机。模仿是对刺激的反应，而不是对刺激的预感。因此，模仿总是"太迟"。刺激动作反应是音乐发展过程中的一个重要部分：

Translations and Keys

要给予儿童方法和时间将内部节奏与外部输入同步。

在另一个例子《一、二》中，儿童可以通过音乐材料：木制节奏棒，来体验大小声，有音乐与无音乐的感觉。在这首歌的结尾"现在我们停下来！"中我们会找到反应的时刻。引导性的实验时间通常被纳入这项活动，使儿童有可能表达自己的音乐意图。学前音乐教育的老师应该密切观察并随着音乐以跟儿童同样的表演方式进行回应。这样，儿童自己就可以发起动作，并在老师的反应中找到肯定的答案。

Keys to Unit Practice

1. Read aloud and write down the following words according to the phonics.

    [bəʊt]　boat　　　　[dʒɔɪn]　join　　　　[fruːt]　fruit
    [bləʊ]　blow　　　　[fuːd]　food　　　　[haʊs]　house

2. Put the school languages into English.

    你有几个玩具？　How many toys do you have?
    谁的书包比较重？　Whose school bag is heavier?
    把长的铅笔拿过来。　Bring the long pencil.
    什么形状像风筝？　What shape looks like a kite?
    把这个圆形涂成蓝色。　Paint this circle blue.
    苹果和香蕉有什么不同？　What is the difference between an apple and a banana?

3. Put the following phrases into Chinese.

    （1）学前儿童音乐教育
    （2）对音乐的动作反应
    （3）通过身体运动理解和感受音乐
    （4）伴随每首歌曲的运动活动
    （5）刺激运动反应

4. Read the blending words and name them.

    telecast　电视广播　　　　cheeseburger　芝士汉堡　　　slimnastics　健美操
    psywarrior　心理战专家　　interpol　国际刑警　　　　　motorcamp　汽车露营
    smog　烟雾　　　　　　　motel　汽车旅馆　　　　　　sitcom　情景喜剧

5. Complete the short passage by filling conjunctions in the blanks.

    One day I was playing the piano （1） when I heard a knock at the door. It was my neighbour Jack. He wanted to buy a second-hand piano. Everyone said I played piano well, （2） so he asked me for help to judge the tone of the piano. We arrived at the owner's house and I looked the piano over, （3） then sat down and played a mixture of honky-tonk numbers （4） and classical pieces. When I finished, I said that the wood was rotten, but （5） still the sound was good and （6） therefore he should buy it.

181

Translation of Extended Reading

音乐运动中心

音乐使幼儿愉快,并吸引他们参与其中。一个装备精良的音乐运动中心是一个幼儿在创造自己音乐的同时进行声音实验的地方。他们获得了对音乐的欣赏和喜爱,这种感受将伴随他们未来的岁月。

> **儿童发展目标**
> 音乐运动中心为促进发展和提高所有发展领域的技能提供许多经验。
> **身体技能:** 提高精细和粗大的运动技能,开发节奏、平衡和空间意识。
> **社交/情感技能:** 提供一种表达感情和情绪的方法,增强自我概念,促进合作和与他人共事,并产生平静和放松的感觉。
> **语言技能:** 提高口语交际能力、词汇量和听力技巧;培养对诗歌和韵律的鉴赏力,增强听觉辨别能力。
> **智力技能:** 培养创造力和想象力,促进解决问题的能力,加强概念开发,鼓励探索,促进发现。

需要记住的几点:

- 音乐可以为课堂设定基调。柔和的音乐能使嘈杂的房间安静下来,而喧闹的音乐会刺激学生。
- 音乐可以激活大脑。把学习设置成音乐,就像《ABC》歌,使学习嵌入更快、层次更深。
- 在转换时期音乐是有效的,比如清理、平静下来,或休息,或准备开始或结束一天。不要把音乐的体验局限在学习中心活动时间。
- 音乐可以成为课堂管理的工具。当说话的声音做不到时,唱歌往往能吸引儿童的注意力。歌谱要包括课堂转换歌曲,让儿童在中心时间唱。
- 音乐可以在圆圈时间以整组、小组和个人的方式体验和欣赏。
- 使用幼儿感觉舒服的音域来唱。
- 让音乐成为自发的、有计划的,或者是另一活动的产物。
- 音乐可以用来创造对其他文化的理解。

建议音乐和运动中心材料投放

CD 播放机和 CD	铃
节奏棒	钹
围巾	钢琴
无线电	歌曲的书籍
歌本	沙锤
玩具麦克风或真麦克风	镜子
带有最喜爱歌曲的歌谱	小地毯
盒式录音机,录像带和空白磁带	多元文化的乐器
鼓	钢琴音乐

Translations and Keys

员工介绍　　　　　　　　　　锻炼支架
服装　　　　　　　　　　　　练习唱片、磁带和视频
吉他　　　　　　　　　　　　书籍
录音机　　　　　　　　　　　期刊
消毒用品　　　　　　　　　　白纸
乐队和管弦乐队的海报　　　　写作用具
舞蹈地毯　　　　　　　　　　舞蹈服装
芭蕾舞鞋　　　　　　　　　　响葫芦
帽子　　　　　　　　　　　　砂块
大的球　　　　　　　　　　　管钟
键盘　　　　　　　　　　　　三角铁
制作乐器的材料　　　　　　　电视
架子隔架　　　　　　　　　　视频播放器
带标签的桶　　　　　　　　　手指镲
练习图　　　　　　　　　　　木琴
练习垫　　　　　　　　　　　踢踏舞鞋
画谜练习卡　　　　　　　　　藤条

183

UNIT 7　Language Development 语言发展

Translation of English Proficiency

语言发展

口头语言和书面语言

　　口头语言就在我们周围，我们认为它是理所当然的，并没有意识到我们所做的选择或我们使用语言的形式。然而，在写作时，书面语言要求有意识地注意形式，这涉及与语义、句法和语音有关的选择。例如，一个四岁刚开始模拟拼写的幼儿想要写"我有一把椅子"，他必须考虑单词的顺序和含义，当他写"椅子"这个单词时，还需要注意到音素，这是他在学习说话时从来没有的。不能低估音素意识的重要性，Richgels（2004）指出，儿童天生就能感知到音素。例如，他们从出生就能感知 /s/ 和 /z/ 在发音上的区别。Richgels（2004）还写道，在口头语言研究中，研究的最大注意力一直是语音，后来甚至主要是在语音学知识的一个分支音素的意识上。

　　口语的句法被认为对阅读启蒙是重要的。有人认为，口语句子建构能力较强的幼儿能为阅读和写作这种新任务带来丰富的语言。《口语记录（ROL）》(Clay et al. 2007) 被开发出来用来测量儿童的句法。然而，在 ROL 的许多句子中有一种结构，它跟使用比较复杂的从属句法结构的书面语言类似。与书面语言不同的是，口语的句法结构更可能是支离破碎的从句和短语串在一起，错误的开头，重复和随意的调群。例如，当一段口语表达与一段朗读出来的书面语表达进行对比时，口语和书面语的区别是明显的。儿童的口语词汇发展是儿童语言习得最明显和最重要的方面之一。一个儿童的词汇量是他或她的语言健康的一个指标，也是他或她在不同的环境中为了多种目的使用语言的能力的一个因素。与在书中朗读的生僻词相比，儿童所听到的日常口语的生僻词少得多。

　　由于口头语言词汇被认为与学习阅读有重要的关联，本研究认为，儿童的词汇量与他们的阅读能力有明确的联系。拥有丰富词汇的儿童被认为是更有效的阅读者。

讨论：口语和阅读学习之间无联系

　　这项对一组 23 名刚上学的儿童进行的小规模研究表明，从口头语言到早期阅读的步骤对于许多儿童来说不是一个按部就班的循序渐进的过程。这项研究提出了许多问题。为什么在口语表达能力方面得分较低的儿童，在上学后的第一年里却成为相对高水平的阅读者呢？为什么口语得分高的儿童还不是高级阅读者呢？为什么有些儿童的口语和阅读能力都很低呢？

　　对此的一个解释是口语和书面语不一样。口语和书面语有不同的词汇、句法和表达机制。下面对口头语言和书面语言的词汇、句法和表达机制进行对比。

表 1　口头语言和书面语言的词汇

口语词汇	书面语词汇
Sit over there.（坐那边。）	Tom sat on the chair.（汤姆坐在椅子上。）
口语是有语境的，依赖于手势，往往是一个句子片段。在书面语言中，主语和宾语是确定的。	

Translations and Keys

在口语中，意思可以通过手势、面部表情和语调来表达，并且名词的发音清晰度可能不重要。然而，在书面语言中，意思必须通过使用明确的语言来实现，主语和宾语按照语法出现在句子中。在口语中，句子片段可能是带着手势的"坐那边"。在书面语句"汤姆坐在椅子上"中，主语"汤姆"以及宾语"椅子"都要明确。

在词汇方面，书面语中的生僻词比口语多。作为一个例子，绘本书《野兽出没的地方》包含生僻字如 "gnashing teeth"（咬牙）和 "terrible roars"（可怕的咆哮）不可能在日常会话中出现。在一系列口语和书面文本的分析中，Hayes 和 Ahrens（1988）揭示了在日常口语每千词中有 17.3 个生僻词；而在儿童书籍每千词中有 30.9 个生僻词——几乎是日常口语的两倍。可能是那些在上学之前家长给他们朗读过书的儿童会接触到更多的生僻词，所以比那些在家里没有听人朗读过书的儿童增加了更多词汇量。关于口语是否映射到书面语的问题，更有可能的是书面语言提供了后来在口语中使用的句法和词汇的范例。

表 2 口头语言和书面语言的句子结构

口语	书面语
We walked for charity on Sunday. 我们星期日去为慈善徒步走。	The Charity Walk will raise money on Sunday. 慈善徒步走将在星期日募捐。
动词转化为名词发生名词化。	
We hid the book. 我们把那本书藏起来了。	The book was hidden. 那本书被藏起来了。
书面语中，宾语放在句首。	
That cat chased a bird. 那只猫追一只鸟。	The cat from next door was chasing a bird. 隔壁那只猫在追一只鸟。
在书面语中，词汇数量增加了，如句子中的名词、形容词、动词和副词等。	

书面语的句法不同于口语的句法。例如，在《野兽出没的地方》一书中，我们读到了 Max who "sailed off through night and day and in and out of weeks"（"他日夜航行，一个星期又一个星期"），这是带有许多词项的一种语言抒情用法。书面语言的句法包含更多从句、直接引语和言说义动词，在下面的例子中，主语 Max 在句子的半路出现，"And now," cried Max, "let the wild rumpus start!"（"现在，"麦克斯喊，"让野兽们闹起来吧！"）

在上面的例子中，"隔壁那只猫在追一只鸟"出自《口语记录（ROL）》(Clay et al. 2007)，是一个比较复杂的句子的例子，更类似于书面语言的句法，而不是口语的句法。

表 3 口头语言和书面语言参考惯例或机制

口语	书面语
声音	字母
语调、重音、音高	标点符号和大写字母，下划线和粗体字体
表示主题变化的表达式，"现在、对、然后"	标题、新页面、段落、章节、像"首先、其次、总结"这样的词语

书面语言包含字母（用来表示声音）、标点和各种字体（用来表示语调、重音和音高）。章节或新观点在书面语中以标题、段落和表示观点顺序的文字来表达，如"首先、其次、最后和总结"。

Attachment: Where the Wild Things Are
附:《野兽出没的地方》

01. In the book, a child named Max is naughty at home, and after being scolded by his mother, he goes to the beast country and has a very interesting adventure.
书中讲述了一名叫 Max 的小孩在家里淘气,被妈妈斥责后,就去了野兽国,经历了非常有趣的冒险。

02. The night, Max wore his wolf suit and made mischief of one kind and another.
那天晚上,麦克斯穿上了他的小狼衣服,做了一个又一个恶作剧。

03. So he was sent to bed without eating anything.
结果妈妈没让他吃晚饭,把他关到了房间里。

Translations and Keys

04. That very night in Max's room a forest grew and grew...
正是在那天晚上，麦克斯的房间里长出了一片树林。长啊长，长啊长……

05. and grew until his ceiling hung with vines
直到天花板上挂满了葡萄藤

06. and the walls became the world all around
墙壁消失在了世界的边缘

07. and an ocean tumbled by with a private boat for Max.
海上漂来了一艘小船。

08. And he sailed off through night and day and in and out of weeks, and almost over a year,
他日夜航行，一个星期又一个星期，几乎用了一年的时间，

09. he came to the place where the wild things are.
他来到这个野兽出没的地方。

187

10. They roared their terrible roars and gnashed their terrible teeth and rolled their terrible eyes and showed their terrible claws
野兽们发出了可怕的咆哮，磨着它们可怕的牙齿，转动着它们可怕的眼睛，伸出了它们可怕的爪子
till Max said "be still!" and tamed with the magic trick of staring into all their yellow eyes without blinking once
"别动！"麦克斯的眼睛一眨也不眨，盯着它们的黄眼睛，用魔法驯服了它们
and they were frightened and called him the most wild thing of all and made him the king of all wild things.
它们全都害怕了，把他当成了野兽之王，现在他成了野兽之王。

11. "And now," cried Max, "let the wild rumpus start!"
　"现在，"麦克斯喊道，"让野兽们闹起来吧！"
"Now stop!" Max said and sent the wild things off to bed without their supper.
　"停！"麦克斯没给它们晚饭就让它们去睡觉了。
And Max, the king of all wild things, was lonely and wanted to be where someone loved him best of all.
可是他这个野兽之王突然感到孤独起来，想到一个被人爱的地方去。

Translations and Keys

Then all around from far away across the world he smelled good things to eat,
这时，从遥远的世界的那一边，飘来了好吃的东西的香味，
so he gave up being king of where the wild things are.
所以他放弃在这个野兽出没的地方当国王了。
Max stepped into his private boat and waved good-bye.
麦克斯上了他的小船，挥手说再见。

12. And he sailed back over a year and in and out of weeks, and through a day
然后他航行了一年，一个星期又一个星期，经过白天

13. and into the night of his very own room where he found his supper waiting for him and it was still hot.
又回到了他自己房间的那个夜晚，他发现他的晚饭正等着他，而饭还是热的。

Keys to Unit Practice

1. Read aloud and write down the following words according to the phonics.

   [ma:kit] __market__   [nə:s] __nurse__   [ʃɔ:t] __short__

   [keə] __care__   [dɪə] __dear__   [auə] __hour__

2. Put the school languages into English.

   你喜欢什么颜色？What colour do you like?/ What's your favorite colour?

   我要画一个苹果。I'm going to draw/paint an apple.

   把纸对折再打开。Fold the paper in half and open it again.

   请把剪刀递给我。Pass me the scissors.

   把你的名字写在画上。Put your name on your painting/drawing.

   请把铅笔放回去。Put the pencil away/back.

3. Put the following phrases and sentences into Chinese.

   （1）语素意识的重要性

   （2）口头和书面语言的句法有区别。

   （3）在口语中，可以通过手势、面部表情和语调来表达意义。

   （4）书面语提供了用于口语的句法和词汇模式。

4. Read the clipping words and name them.

   gas 气体，汽油   bus 公共汽车   lunch 午餐
   memo 备忘录   cab 出租车   Dept   部门
   gent 男厕所，先生   ad   广告   kilo   公斤（千克）

5. Rewrite the sentences according to the tips in the bracket.

   （1）It was very strange that she should have said that. (using the infinitive)

   It was very strange __for her to have said__ that.

   （2）The idea is that we should meet on Thursday. (using the infinitive)

   The idea is __for us to meet__ on Thursday.

   （3）I'm surprised to find it easy that they will work on it in a short time. (using the infinitive)

   I'm surprised to find it easy __for them to work__ on it in a short time.

   （4）The girl opened the door so that the little cat could go out. (using the infinitive)

   The girl opened the door __for the little cat to go out__.

   （5）It was a pleasure that I had been invited to my best friend's wedding. (using the infinitive)

   It was a pleasure __for me to have been invited__ to my best friend's wedding.

   （6）That Jack didn't get to the station on time made all of us worried. (using the gerund)

   __Jack's not getting to__ the station on time made all of us worried.

   （7）My worry is that you rely too much on your parents. (using the gerund)

Translations and Keys

My worry is <u>your relying</u> too much on your parents.

（8）Would you mind if I opened the window for a little while? (using the gerund)

Would you mind <u>my opening</u> the window for a little while?

Translation of Extended Reading

读写中心

通过读写中心，孩子们练习阅读、书写和拼写的基本技能。他们有机会在独立活动或小组活动的时候加强和拓展这些技能。读写中心的活动能够使孩子们自信地向成为成功的阅读者和交流者前进。

儿童发展目标

读写中心为促进发展和提高所有发展领域的技能提供许多经验。

身体技能： 加强眼手协调、精细运动技能、视觉辨别和听觉辨别技能。

社交/情感技能： 培养合作、自控、自尊和自信。

语言技能： 发展对声音和印刷文字在交流中的重要性的理解力，积累词汇，声音记忆能力，理解能力，听力技巧和语言表达能力。

智力技能： 提供说出名称、辨别、回想、预测、排序、模仿、决策和创造的机会。

需要记住的几点：

- 明确界定读写中心的范围。
- 改变活动以维持和激发兴趣。
- 提供多层次的活动，以适应儿童的能力。
- 一次介绍一种教具，解释并示范设备及用品的护理和操作方法。
- 提供学生责任的制度。
- 儿童专注从事一些有意义的活动，如制作菜单、收集电话号码或写原创故事。

建议读写中心教具材料投放

各种大小和类型的书籍　　　　磁带录音机和空白磁带

杂志和报纸　　　　　　　　　磁带播放器

口袋图书　　　　　　　　　　广告，教师创作和学生创作的磁带

句子条　　　　　　　　　　　语音电话

用于分类的图片、文字和物体　挂图（包括姓名、字母表、环境词语、童

字母块、邮票和印台　　　　　谣和诗歌）

书写材料　　　　　　　　　　磁性字母和板

带有图片、字母和文字的法兰绒板　作者的椅子

阅读室指针和"眼镜"　　　　八页迷你书

常见单词列表
图片词典
壁纸样品
简单的单词搜索
打孔机
班级名单列表
图
网格
维恩图
故事地图
手翻书
盘垫
冰棒棍
日记
游戏
投影机
贺卡
滑动面具或标志
故事提示
手语图
橡皮泥
字母和数字切割机
计算机
纸币和硬币
带名字的学校员工海报
沙盘

盐盘
学生自制书用的空白书
纸类
蜡笔、记号笔、钢笔、铅笔
有趣或不寻常的书写用具
地图
放大镜
标签
信封
食谱
菜单
邮箱
铭牌
笔记本
打字机
期刊
订书机
便签
纱线
鞋带
剪贴板——正规尺寸和微缩的
带切孔苍蝇拍
用于指针或滑动面具的模切机
白板和白板笔
清管器

Translations and Keys

UNIT 8　Teacher Handbook 教师手册

Translation of English Proficiency

学生能力评估

书写发展阶段

　　早期书写技巧的发展是儿童早期读写能力培养的另一个方面。以下阶段都代表着儿童书写发展的不同阶段。所有阶段都是重叠的，儿童在不同的年龄阶段都会进步并达到不同的书写阶段。不管你的孩子处于哪个阶段，都可以通过鼓励定期书写来加强写作能力的发展。儿童永远不应该被阻止用他们能够做的方式来探索写作，无论是涂鸦、字母串、自创的拼写，还是常规的拼写。

阶段	示例
无文字阶段：图画 • 使用绘画作为交流的手段 • 相信绘画和书写是有目的的信息交流方式 • 阅读他们的图画，就好像他们在写东西一样	
无文字阶段：涂鸦 • 涂鸦，但把它当成书写 • 效仿书写 • 像成人一样握笔和用笔	
早期书写：类字母形式 • 书写的形状实际上类似字母 • 形状不是真的字母 • 看起来就像蹩脚的字母，却是独特的创造	

续表

阶段	示例
初期：随意的字母或字母串 • 使用字母序列，可能从他们的名字中学来的 • 可能用多种方式写同一个字母 • 随机排列的长字母串	CHPFD PE3dP4 NC rmS O2td/
过渡：自创的拼写 • 在不知道常规拼写的情况下创建自己的拼写 • 一个字母可能代表整个音节 • 单词可能重叠 • 可能不会使用适当的间距 • 随着书写的成熟，更多的单词能规范地书写 • 随着书写的成熟，可能只有一两个字母自创或省略了	I wl b hape wen skul iz t I lk t pla wt mi fredz in te Sumr tatz itz ov fn
流畅：规范的拼写 • 通常类似于成年人的书写	Once upon a time a dog named Rags got ost n the woods. A of the people ooked for him After a wh e he found his way home again H s fam y was very happy

语音意识

说听技能为识字提供了基础。研究表明，儿童的阅读成果可以通过他们的早期语言能力来预测。有些儿童可能需要特别学习语音意识技能。语音意识是对声音的感知和对单词以下特质的领悟：

能够被分解成多个音节，如 (hos-pit-al)；

有韵律，如 (can, fan, man)；

可以以同样的发音开始，如 (never, naughty)；

可以被分解成第一个发音或第一组发音和韵式，如 (s-and) (st-and)；

可以将不同的单音组合在一起形成单词，如 (f-i-s-h or f-ish makes fish)；

可以被分成单音，如 (s-a-n-d)；

可以通过添加、删除或重新排序来改变发音，从而创造新的单词，

如（加 s，sand 变成 and；把 a 改成 e，sand 变成 send）

培养语音意识的活动

朗读以下故事书：

- *Each, Peach, Pear, Plum,* Janet & Alan Ahlberg

- *Goodness Gracious,* Phil Cummings

- *Where's my Teddy?* Jez Alborough

- *Don't forget the Bacon,* Pat Hutchins

- *Pass the Jam Jim,* Kaye Umansky & Margaret Chamberlain

Translations and Keys

- *Animalia,* Graeme Base
- *Can You Hear Me Grandad?* Pat Thompson.

在儿童熟悉这个故事之后，鼓励他们在每个句子的结尾都找出押韵的词，例如："Hairy Mclairy from Donaldson's... " 和 "Hercules Morse as big as a ... "

做以下游戏和活动：

- 拍手和演奏乐器说出：el-e-phant, Is-a-bell-a
- 作为日常活动的一部分，儿童按照他们名字中的音节数来分组，如："如果你的名字有3个音节，那就去领午餐吧。"
- 组成韵律，如：man, fan, pan, Dan。
- 用韵脚来匹配物品/图片，如：house/mouse, dog/log。
- 采用韵头来把儿童的名字编成一句话，如：Sally slides slowly, Joshua jumps, Billy bounces.
- 发音桶游戏。拿出一个物体，说出它的名字，然后找到它的第一个发音。想出另一个以同样的发音开始的单词。桶里还有其他东西是以相同发音开头的吗？
- 发音篮子或桌子。桌子上或篮子里的所有物件都必须是以同一个字母开头的。
- 字母商店。挑选一个字母，然后看看商店里能出售多少以这个字母开头的东西，如：L商店有 lollies, lettuce, licorice, lasagna, lemons。

握笔阶段

最新的研究表明，只要能使用并且能握稳，任何握笔方式都是可以接受的，即铅笔不滑落，孩子能控制，写字不累。

1. 手掌抓法

第一阶段
铅笔夹在手掌上，握住顶端。铅笔尖朝下，大拇指朝上。

第二阶段
铅笔是用一边的拇指和另一边所有手指握住，掌心向下。

2. 三角式握法

第一阶段
随着孩子的成长和发育，从抓到握的过程逐渐进步。铅笔夹在拇指与食指之间。中指伸到笔杆下面，或沿手指侧支撑铅笔。
总的来说，对铅笔尖有了更多的控制，但仍在使用整个手臂的动作来控制，几乎没有对手的小肌肉的控制。

第二阶段
再一次，逐渐有了进步。在握笔的第二阶段，由于肩、肘和腕的固定姿势变得更加稳定，所以较少出现整个手臂的动作。

3. 成熟握法

拇指和食指相抵夹住铅笔靠在中指上。由拇指和食指的精细小动作进行控制。无名指和小拇指加固中指。

Keys to Unit Practice

1. Read aloud and write down the following words according to the phonics.

   [mauθ] mouth   [ðɪs] this   [wi:l] wheel

   [pæk] pack   [kætʃ] catch   [ʃi:p] sheep

2. Put the school languages into English.

   吃饭前请洗手。Please wash your hands before you eat.

   洗手后记得关水龙头。Remember to turn off the tap after washing.

   再喝点水吧。Please drink more water.

   汤别洒了。Don't spill the soup.

   多吃点水果。Have more fruit.

   别急，慢慢享用。Take your time. Enjoy your meal.

3. Put the following into Chinese.

   （1）儿童早期读写能力发展

   （2）使用绘画作为沟通的手段

   （3）语音意识能力

   （4）单词可以分解成音节。

   （5）听说能力是读写的基础。

4. Read the acronyms and name them.

   TOEFL 托福考试   AIDS 艾滋病   GDP 国内生产总值

   CD 光盘   DVD 数字化视频光盘   IT 信息技术

   VIP 贵宾   IQ 智商   EQ 情商

5. Choose the best answer to complete the sentences.

   （1）D。现在分词独立主格作原因状语。其逻辑主语与句子主语不一致。

   （2）B。There be 句型的独立主格结构，在句中作原因状语。

   （3）A。过去分词的独立主格结构，其逻辑主语和与句子主语不一致，且动词 settle 与其逻辑主语是动宾关系，所以用过去分词。

   （4）B。现在分词的独立主格作伴随状语。当逻辑主语是人的身体部位时，如果动词是及物动词，用过去分词；如果是不及物动词，用现在分词。

   例：The boy lay on the ground, his eyes closed and his hands trembling.

   （5）B。考查非谓语动词，即独立主格结构。题干中有逗号，且无连词，首先排除 A。根据 at the end of last March，排除 C（正在进行）和 D（将来动作）项，表示动作完成故选 B。

   （6）C。B 项缺连词，不正确。D 项语态有误。A 项干扰大。若选 A，则 the work 就成了 given 的逻辑主语，整个句子就变成了：If the work is given more time, the work can be done much better. 这样一来，也就是 give the work more time，显然不合逻辑，实际上应该是 give sb. more

Translations and Keys

time，因此 A 项是错误的。C 项是正确的。其中分词 given 另有自己的逻辑主语 more time。这种自带主语的分词结构被称为"分词的独立主格"。其作用相当于状语从句：If more time is given (to us), the work can be done much better.

（7）A。从所给的四个选项来看，do 的逻辑主语是 his homework 且为动宾关系，故选 A。这个句子也可用介词 with 的复合结构来表示：With his homework done, he went and watched the game. D 项时态错误。C 项 doing 表示主动，不对。B 项 done 与主语 he 矛盾。若改为 Having done his homework，正确。

（8）C。过去分词独立主格作时间状语，其逻辑主语与动词 finish 是动宾关系，所以用过去分词。

Translation of Extended Reading

写作中心

儿童爱写字，并且喜欢给任何愿意听的人读他们写的东西。写作中心让儿童有机会在各种不同的经历中通过写作进行交流。写作中心鼓励儿童早期的写作兴趣，并为他们开始写作的努力和写作的愿望提供了基础。

儿童发展目标

写作中心为促进发展和提高所有发展领域的技能提供许多经验。

身体技能：提高精细运动技能，发展视觉辨别能力，发展手眼协调能力。

社交/情感技能：鼓励表达感情和情感，培养对他人写作的欣赏，促进合作，团队意识，分享和协作。

语言技能：提高口语交际能力和词汇量，发展拼写、语音技能，理解写作目的，增强阅读能力。

智力技能：培养思考、推理、质疑、创造力和想象力，并提高解决问题的能力。

需要记住的几点：

- 建立具有明确界限的区域。
- 示范正确使用教具材料的方法。
- 提供各种现实的、有目的的写作素材。
- 添加补充的物品和道具，以加强写作和当前主题。
- 备有儿童展示写作作品的地方。
- 在受儿童邀请的情况下，参与他们的写作，并做示范。鼓励儿童把他们写的东西读给你或其他人听。
- 使用标签和图片标明物品属于哪里，以便于清理。
- 创建一个识字加强中心，配有词卡、词墙、词典和适当的书籍。
- 保持教具材料良好的使用状态，例如更换干了的白板笔。
- 征募成年志愿者，来帮助完成出版任务。

建议写作中心教具材料投放

铅笔	砂和盐盘
钢笔	词墙
粉笔和黑板	班级名单
魔术石板	字母条
醋酸片	日期邮票
订书机	电脑
浆糊或胶水	桌子或书桌
卷笔刀	数字邮票
办公用品	期刊
彩色铅笔	写作提示
蜡笔	办公室游戏、卡片店和邮局的道具
字母邮票	从医生或牙医诊所打印材料
信和设计模板	白板和白板笔
打孔机	带格线的拼写簿
磁带	画架
信封和卡片	笔记本
白板笔	便利贴
印台	文件夹
索引卡	标签/贴纸
剪刀	纱线
旧杂志	清管器
字母表	加法机带
书籍装订材料	通心粉和意大利面
图片字典	荧光笔
纸	图片提示
邮箱	单词搜索

References

[1] 刘霞. 幼儿园英语口语大全 [M]. 北京：清华大学出版社，2005.

[2] 高敬. 幼师英语 [M]. 上海：华东师范大学出版社，2013.

[3] 姚丹，李章华，黄芳. 幼儿教师实用英语口语（中级）[M]. 上海：复旦大学出版社，2012.

[4] 王桂珍. 英语语音教程 [M]. 北京：高等教育出版社，2005.

[5] 张志远. 儿童英语教学法 [M]. 北京：外语教学与研究出版社，2002.

[6] 张荣斌. 新编儿童英语教学技能 [M]. 北京：北京邮电大学出版社，2014.

[7] 杨文，宋占美. 学前教育专业英语 [M]. 北京：北京师范大学出版社，2011.

[8] 强海燕，赵琳，Linda Siegei. 幼儿英语浸入式教育 [M]. 西安：西安交通大学出版社，2000.

[9] https://www.unicef.org/

[10] https://www.education.gov.au/

[11] http://www.preschoolrainbow.org/activities-circle.htm

[12] http://www.yingyu.com/e/20140916/5417e8b828455.shtml

[13] https://wenku.baidu.com/view/00c89c32f011f18583d049649b6648d7c1c70827.html

[14] http://yuer.hujiang.com

[15] https://st.hujiang.com/topic/165281479398/

[16] https://www.goodreads.com/author/quotes/15332.Rachel_Carson

[17] https://www.douban.com/note/576675573/

[18] http://www.yingyuyufa.com/